Jimmy Stewart
A Life in Film

Jimmy Stewart
A Life in Film

ROY PICKARD

St. Martin's Press
New York

Library of Congress Cataloging-in-Publication Data

Pickard, Roy.
    Jimmy Stewart : a life in film / Roy Pickard.
       p.   cm.
    "A Thomas Dunne book."
    Filmography: p.
    ISBN 0-312-08828-0
    1. Stewart, James, 1908–   . 2. Motion picture actors and actresses—United States—Biography. I. Title.
  PN2287.S68P53   1993
  791.43′028′092—dc20
  [B]   92-36316
                                       CIP

First published in Great Britain by Robert Hale Limited.

First U.S. Edition: January 1993
10 9 8 7 6 5 4 3 2 1

Contents

List of Illustrations

8

PICTURE CREDITS

The illustrations in this book come from the stills issued to publicize films made or distributed by the following companies:

Columbia: 1, 2, 15, 20, 21, 22; MGM: 3; National General Pictures: 26; Paramount: 13, 14, 16, 17, 18, 19, 27; RKO: 4; 20th Century Fox: 7, 10, 24; Universal: 8, 9, 11, 12, 23, 25; Warner Brothers: 5, 6.

Although every effort has been made to trace the copyright holders of photographs, the publishers apologize in advance for any unintentional omission or neglect and will be pleased to insert the appropriate acknowledgement to the companies or individuals concerned in any subsequent edition of this book.

Introduction

For almost his entire career Jimmy Stewart has presented himself as an ordinary guy, the kind of man that people could believe in. Men liked him because they could relate to him. They saw something of themselves reflected in his screen persona. If he found himself in a dangerous situation, holding on for dear life in a Hitchcock film or up against corrupt politicians, they would say to themselves: 'Yeah, I probably would have done that … I guess I might have acted that way,' and they found that reassuring. Jimmy Stewart was a guy they felt they knew!

It was the same with women. To them, Stewart's long beanpole frame, his kind, gentle, puzzled image, his shy hesitancy as he stumbled over and searched for words, was far more attractive and real than the phonier pretty boy glamour of some of the more obvious Hollywood stars.

Today, Jimmy Stewart is well into his eighties, but the spry charm and appeal still holds good. Question a young woman in her late teens or early twenties about the stars of old and it's likely that you'll get a groan about 'all those old black and white movies'. But Jimmy Stewart? That's different. 'Oh yes,' they say, following it up with just a simple 'yes' and allowing their warm smiles and the one single word to say it all.

Of all the male Hollywood stars who flourished in the golden age, Stewart is the one who has survived the longest. No actor has seen quite so many changes and yet so convincingly held on to his stature and stardom. His slow, amiable 'Mr Ordinary Citizen', complete with the chin rubbing embarrassment, the 'aw shucks ma'am' drawl, the false starts, apologetic gestures and throat-catching earnestness have helped make him an indestructible legend. For many he has always been the same, always Jimmy Stewart.

Sentences that start out with: 'Waal ... I guess ... I'll ... just ... er ... have to think er ... ' have become so familiar that they tend to make audiences believe that Stewart is not really acting at all. So relaxed and easy going is he on screen that his talent is taken for granted. There is, however, much more to Stewart than meets the eye and the accusation that Jimmy Stewart simply plays himself begs the question: 'Exactly which Jimmy Stewart do you mean?'

The honest young idealist fighting corruption in *Mr Smith Goes to Washington* or the gentle alcoholic who finds solace with an invisible giant rabbit in *Harvey*? The vengeful loner of the Anthony Mann westerns or the San Francisco cop obsessed with the memory of a dead love in *Vertigo*? The voyeur with a telescope in a Manhattan apartment in *Rear Window* or the humble but inwardly shrewd country lawyer in *Anatomy of a Murder*? There are an awful lot of Stewarts there. And none of them is the same.

There is a subtlety to Stewart's acting and also an incredible flexibility. Once the outward veneer of his homespun All-American image has been stripped away there is an alert, complex, highly intelligent performer, a man who has brought sincerity and conviction to even the humblest role. His voice remains one of the most appealing and durable in the history of movies. It has both range and richness. It can be harsh, even laced with sarcasm on occasion and at times melancholy and resigned, but when used to address women, it is gentle, kind and sometimes tremulous as Stewart shows amazement that such creatures actually exist.

Stewart has been called by no less a critic than Andrew Sarris, 'the most complete actor-personality in the American cinema'. For more than forty years the most talented of Hollywood directors sought his services: Capra, Hitchcock, Ford, Wilder, Stevens, Preminger, Borzage, Lubitsch, Cukor, Mann, Hathaway. For them and audiences the world over he was 'Mr Everyman', not 'everyman of distinction' but 'every (average) man', the guy with his roots in small-town America, the son of God-fearing parents, the personification of everything that was honest, decent and respectable.

That Stewart should come to represent such values was by no means surprising for it was in a small American town – Indiana, Pennsylvania (population: approx 6,000) – that he was born, on 20 May 1908, and grew up in the early years of the century. As a boy he lived with his parents and two sisters, went to school and helped out in his father's hardware store. He did nothing remarkable and nothing remarkable happened to him. There was certainly no hint that he would become an actor. Instead, just before enrolling at Princeton, he considered a military career or even something in some way tied up with flying. After Princeton and with a Bachelor of Science degree to his name he dabbled with the possibility of becoming an architect.

It was only when one of his Princeton pals, Joshua Logan, asked him to spend a summer at West Falmouth on Cape Cod that he thought of giving acting a go. Logan ran a summer stock company called The University Players. Hank Fonda, Margaret Sullavan, Mildred Natwick, Myron McCormick and others acted there. Together, they convinced Stewart that he had talent and should join them in New York. 'It was like getting bitten by a malaria mosquito,' said Stewart as he found, to his surprise, that he was indeed rather good at acting and that performing on stage came to him rather easily. Better still, he actually enjoyed it.

Broadway saw him for just three years in a handful of plays including *Goodbye Again, Spring in Autumn, Yellow Jack* and *Divided by Three* with Judith Anderson. Most of the plays were quickly forgotten, but Stewart was not. Thanks to MGM talent scout Bill Grady, Hollywood beckoned and just seven years after starting out at Princeton, Stewart found himself heading for Los Angeles and an uncertain future.

What happened when Stewart eventually arrived in Hollywood and began a career that was to rank with the most distinguished in movie history makes up the pages of this book. In many ways it is a double story: the tale of a fine actor and the tale of the extraordinary community in which he worked – a place that was at once colourful and bizarre, tawdry and glamorous, filled to the brim with mediocrity and overflowing with talent.

The book derives from two interviews I conducted with Mr Stewart – the first when he arrived in London in 1975 to appear in *Harvey*, the second in the eighties when he was on a promotional tour for the re-release of five classic Alfred Hitchcock films, including four he'd made with the director in the forties and fifties. It also includes passages from subsequent interviews made in Hollywood with people who knew and worked with Stewart during his long career – Frank Capra, one lazy afternoon at La Quinta, near Palm Springs, Bette Davis, Henry Hathaway, Cornel Wilde, Charlton Heston, Carroll Baker, Rock Hudson, Henry Koster, producer Joe Pasternak, Lee Remick, Otto Preminger, Robert Aldrich, Lee J. Cobb, William Wyler, Andrew McLaglen and, of course, Hank Fonda.

This then is the story of a genuine American hero – one of the nicest of nice guys. On screen what made him so likeable was that he refused to be fazed by urban sophistication or hustled into a lifestyle that didn't suit him. He was never brash, corrupt or egotistical. To the natural losers of this world he brought the comforting message that the cynics, slick talkers and crooks would not inherit the earth, at least not as long as he was around.

It is the story of a man who considered his job well done if he could get through a film 'and not have the acting show'.

Like many Hollywood movies, it begins with a flashback ...

1 Hollywood 1980

'How the hell did he get to be so good?
I've been in awe of him ever since.'
Henry Fonda

The American Film Institute chairman Charlton Heston
was the first to arrive, smiling his way through the jostling
crowds, the waves, the smiles, the TV cameras. Next came
Grace Kelly, resplendent in blue. Then a smiling Bill
Holden with Stefanie Powers, a crumpled Walter
Matthau, Jack Lemmon, Gene Kelly, Karl Malden, George
Kennedy ... and from the modern generation, the
diminutive Dustin Hoffman.

The venue was the Beverly Hills Hilton in Hollywood.
The date, February 28, 1980. The occasion, The American
Film Institute Life Achievement Award. The recipient, a
star who for forty-five years had been entertaining the
world with his skilful artistry and the deceptive simplicity
of his acting – Jimmy Stewart.

Inside the luxury ballroom, the murmur and babble of
the guests faded as the lights dimmed and a huge screen
flickered into life presenting a huge close-up of Stewart's
face, gentle, kindly, half-smiling. He said softly, 'My name
is Dowd, Elwood P. ...'.

From *Harvey* the image changed to *The Spirit of St Louis*.
Now it was heroic. 'My name is Lindbergh' Cut. Stewart
again, in *Anatomy of a Murder*, pleading, wide-eyed, arms
outstretched. Small-town, All-American. 'Your honour I'm
just a simple country lawyer.'

And so it went on, each scene being greeted with
applause until the montage finally came to an end and
Stewart's face froze on the huge screen. The scene was

13

from Frank Capra's *It's a Wonderful Life.*

'I want you to take a good look at that face,' said a voice on the soundtrack.

'Who is it?' came the reply.

'That's George Bailey.'

'Hmm ... it's a good face. I like it.'

Applause again, prolonged this time as the lights were raised and an off-stage announcement said simply: 'From Beverly Hills, California, The American Film Institute salute to James Stewart'. And then everyone was standing as the tall, gangling, 72-year-old grey haired figure entered the room to the strains of 'Shenandoah', clasping the outstretched hands, smiling broadly as he walked swiftly and erect to the top table. For a second he stood and waved, his hand acknowledging the applause. Then after a kiss for his wife Gloria and for Grace Kelly, he took his seat and waited for the 'ordeal' to begin.

It was Hank Fonda who got things under way. Master of Ceremonies for the evening he strolled to the podium, a broad grin across his face. He knew the tensions only too well. They got to even the most hardened of performers. Just two years earlier he himself had been honoured. For an instant he indulged in a moment of malicious delight. He waved: 'Glad it's you Jim ... in the hot seat. Gloria, hold his hand and make him enjoy it.'

Then it began in earnest: the flashbacks to the early small town life in Indiana, Pennsylvania; how Stewart had made it from Princeton to Broadway; how Fonda had known him for more than fifty years. 'Jimmy never seemed to go out to look for work,' he said. 'It just happened. I'd been walking the pavements for five years. How the hell did he get to be so good. I've been in awe of him ever since. I treasure every moment, Jim.'

The lights faded again. Another montage. This time Stewart in *Born To Dance*, with Margaret Sullavan in *Shopworn Angel*, in the western *Destry Rides Again*, with Cary Grant in *The Philadelphia Story*, back West again in Ford's *The Man Who Shot Liberty Valance*.

As Stewart watched, the images seemed to merge. Faces he had known for more than half a century stared back at him, some from the screen, some half hidden in darkness in the audience. The faces told him that it really had been forty-five years. So too did the memory of those faces that were missing and were no longer part of his life. His longtime friend and agent Leland Hayward. The lovely Margaret Sullavan, Coop, director John Ford, Tracy, Anthony Mann ... All gone.

His eyes refocused on Hank Fonda who was continuing in his praise. He more than anyone reminded him of what it had been like and of the eager anticipation and excitement he had felt when he had landed by plane in Hollywood in the summer of 1935, a thousand movies ago.

2 Small Parts in Big Films, Big Parts in Small Films

'I told him to forget the camera … In his
very first scene he showed he had all the
good things.'

Spencer Tracy

It couldn't really have been a better start. A chance to
work in Hollywood after just three years on Broadway,
the opportunity to test if the acting bug that had been
nagging him for years was for real, and a $350 a week
contract at Hollywood's biggest studio, MGM.

When Jimmy Stewart stepped off the plane in Los
Angeles in June 1935, he counted himself as one of the
luckiest guys alive, and the ensuing days and weeks were
no let-down. Metro was everything he had expected it to
be, the Grand Hotel of Hollywood Studios – luxurious,
spacious and resplendent. Former junk tycoon Louis B.
Mayer ruled the lot; the gifted young Irving Thalberg was
his first lieutenant, supervising all the key productions
through their various stages and ensuring that Metro
represented the very best in elegance and taste.

Seventeen directors transferred the Mayer-Thalberg
visions to the screen. More than fifty screenwriters toiled
on scripts that bristled with slick repartee, and some sixty
stars and contract players brought it all to life on the
screen. There were 4000 employees at Culver City. Stewart
had joined the biggest repertory company in the world.
There were, he quickly discovered, both advantages and
drawbacks. The advantages were obvious – everything on
tap whenever you needed it. MGM catered for every
emergency. The main drawback was the huge roster of

16

male stars that loomed up ahead of him, each and every one effectively blocking any chance of a quick rise to the top. Clark Gable, Spencer Tracy, William Powell, Robert Montgomery, Franchot Tone and others had first call on the studio's top roles. Actors such as the 27-year-old Stewart were required to work their way up, either through appearing in supporting roles in Metro's starry productions or by taking the lead in the occasional B movie.

One theory often mooted around the studio commissary by newcomers was that it didn't really matter what you appeared in as long as you shared a key scene (or scenes) with a major star, preferably a female star. That way you were bound to get noticed. The 'key-scene theory' didn't seem to work too well for other newcomers at MGM. John Beal, Alan Curtis and Eric Linden all struggled to get a foothold. It did work though for Stewart. In his first film *Murder Man* he got to share scenes with Spencer Tracy. It was a routine movie. Stewart had a bit as a gangling newspaperman called Shorty. The picture wasn't much, but Tracy was Tracy. Spencer said: 'I told him to forget the camera was there. That was all he needed. In his very first scene he showed he had all the good things.'

The luck stayed with Stewart. In his second movie he starred with Nelson Eddy and Jeanette MacDonald in a version of the operetta *Rose Marie*. They sang. He acted. As opera singer MacDonald's brother on the run for the murder of a mountie he got noticed. His biggest break, however, occurred with his fourth film *Wife vs. Secretary*. The picture was a formula romantic comedy of the kind that MGM put together with consummate ease during the thirties – magazine editor Clark Gable loves wife Myrna Loy, but has a flirtation with secretary Jean Harlow. Stewart was sixth on the cast list. His role was that of Harlow's fiance. He had only a few scenes in the picture. The highlight was a kissing scene with Harlow which was shot at night. Harlow took one look at Stewart, said to herself 'yes please' and then proceeded to make the most of her opportunities. Stewart, shy and hesitant at first, responded. His education if not his acting ability increased ten-fold in the ensuing half hour. Stewart remembered the scene well: He said:

> It was high voltage stuff. Harlow's role in the film was that of an ambitious secretary – at least that's what they called her in the picture. I had this scene with her. We sat in an automobile while I told her my plans. The scene ended with a kiss.
>
> The lines weren't much and neither of us paid much attention to them but in the first rehearsal, she took charge of the kissing. It was then that I knew I'd never really been kissed before.
>
> There were six rehearsals. The kissing gained each time in interest and enthusiasm. By the time we actually shot the scene my psychology was all wrinkled. She was a stunning girl with a dress so low cut you had to bend down to pick it up. And me? I was just a guy from Pennsylvania. She had that platinum hair and beautiful face. And she slouched. Slinking was fashionable then. Her dresses were tight. She wore nothing under them. Shooting that scene made it quite a night!

Anything that Harlow did on screen made news, and the Harlow kiss helped Stewart gain that little extra attention in Hollywood. She was the first major female star he'd appeared with. Once again he got noticed, this time by the critic of the London *Observer* who wrote: 'What I liked best about this picture was the performance of Mr James Stewart as the secretary's fiance. He is one of the young moderns of whom you feel with a start of surprise, that good actors don't stop with your own generation – they keep right along coming.'

Which was, of course, why MGM had hired him in the first place. Since 1924, when Metro had first been formed, the studio's policy had always been to have as many stars on their books as possible. They were never satisfied with the word 'enough'. Their proud boast was that they had under contract 'More Stars Than There Were In Heaven'. Stewart was simply another addition to the already star-studded line-up. Not yet a star, but hopefully one in the not too distant future.

The work rate during Stewart's first year at Metro was scorching – six days a week for fifty-two weeks a year. Stewart did everything, small parts in big films, big parts in small films. Sometimes he would be on a picture for just two or three days. On other occasions he would be required for three weeks. There would also be times when he would leave a film temporarily, complete a part in another picture, and then return to finish the film he had been working on earlier. There were also periods when he would have three or four films on the go at once, and if there was a gap in his schedule he was not allowed to remain idle. The studio claimed him for screen tests. He did more than 500. Only the back of his head was seen as he talked to a beautiful girl having her first screen test.

L.B. Mayer oversaw everything, from tests to previews and premieres. His preference was for warm, sentimental stories. Family entertainment was his motto. So too was 'Make It Good … Make It Big … Give It Class! With the help of Thalberg, he made sure his films lived up to it. The melodramas, the comedies and the musicals *were* good. They *were* big and thanks to the extravagant sets of Cedric Gibbons, the lavish gowns of Adrian and the shimmering camerawork of Oliver Marsh, William Daniels, Joseph Ruttenberg and others they *did* have class.

In the mid-thirties Mayer was way out ahead of everyone in the movie world, a celluloid king on a salary of a million dollars a year. Many despised him. One screenwriter commented: 'I'd rather have TB than LB.' But there were also those who swore that he was not the ogre he was so often made out to be. Robert Taylor's view was that he was a kind, fatherly, understanding and protective man. Joan Crawford was also pro-Mayer: 'I was free to go to him for advice of any kind at any time. He was patient with people, had great judgment and didn't play games.' On the other hand, when child star Elizabeth Taylor joined Metro in the forties she referred to the MGM chief as a dwarf with a big nose!

Stewart said: 'I didn't see too much of him to start with. I was, after all, only a contract player, but we were treated very well. They took you under their wing and you worked all the time. They protected you if you got into a scrape. They fixed your teeth and gave you voice lessons. They got you new clothes and took care of your publicity. It was a wonderful training ground. If they hadn't paid me I think I would have paid them.'

Hank Fonda didn't share Stewart's enthusiasm for the glitter of Hollywood. He was at a different studio, the newly formed 20th Century-Fox. There, the amenities were less luxurious. The studio was struggling to make a name for itself. Fonda had leading roles but he didn't like any of them, and he regarded filming as slumming. He would have preferred to have been back in New York, acting on Broadway. He grumbled: 'You go to the studio having learned three pages of script. Then you act three minutes a day in front of the cameras. Its not very exacting and its not very important. You do as many takes as the director wants and that's it. Then you go home.' Neither was Fonda much impressed by the directors who were supposed to be guiding him: 'Most of 'em are satisfied if nothing goes wrong. If you say all the words, look intelligent and nobody drops a hammer you get by.' Then he would look at Stewart and shake his head: 'This ain't an actor's town Jimmy.'

It was, however, very much a fun town. For all his grumbles about having to work in Hollywood Fonda was not slow to indulge in its nightly pleasures. He knew exactly where the best nightclubs were located, where the best parties were held and where the prettiest girls could be found.

Stewart had shacked up with Fonda at a Mexican-styled farmhouse in Brentwood and was not slow to join in on the nightly escapades. There were plenty of dates – and also double dates, notably with Lucille Ball (Fonda) and Ginger Rogers (Stewart) with the latter doing her best to teach an awkward Stewart the intricacies of The Carioca. Of the four Stewart usually came out of things the best. Ginger did the teaching, Fonda the cooking and a dejected Lucille Ball the washing up. Stewart just tried to dance.

There were also parties – some were good, some were wild and others were disastrous. A house-party held by producer Walter Wanger fell into the latter category. Held partly to promote his next movie it was attended by both

Stewart and Fonda and also Humphrey Bogart who was another star to have recently arrived from Broadway. Eight of the loveliest 'models' in the world were on hand. All were scheduled to appear in Wanger's movie. They looked ready for anything – they chewed gum, wore dangling rhinestone earrings and were sheathed in clinging satin backless evening gowns. Bogart couldn't believe his eyes. He had been hoping for a roll in the hay, but took one look at the girls and commented: 'Anyone who would sleep with one of those girls would throw a rock through a Rembrandt.' Shortly thereafter he left. So did Stewart and Fonda who were also able to resist temptation. The eight magnolia petals duly appeared in the Wanger movie. Like the party it flopped.

Closer to home Stewart and Fonda decided that it was about time they met up with the legendary Greta Garbo. She lived next door but had kept herself to herself by erecting a high white fence between the two gardens. Fonda couldn't believe that Stewart had never come across her at Metro. They worked at the same studio for God's sake. Nope, said Stewart, he had never seen her. Determined to put things to rights they hatched a plan to tunnel under their garden and into that of the star who, even then, wanted to be alone.

Stewart later recalled that they had to abandon the tunnel when they encountered some obstacles such as a gas main or a sewage pipe. Fonda maintained that he had wanted to continue, but that Stewart gave up. Stewart said it was the other way round. Whatever the truth of the matter, the tunnel was barely half dug and both men finished up having consumed large amounts of alcohol in the process. 'It was damned hard work', said Fonda. 'I wanted to meet Garbo, but even she wasn't worth that amount of effort.' Garbo didn't stay in any case. Shortly afterwards she moved to another part of Hollywood.

The constant whirl of hectic social activity was such that at least one old acquaintance from the Broadway stage, Joshua Logan, thought the pair had 'Gone Hollywood' when he arrived in Los Angeles in 1935. Logan's profile wasn't quite as high as the two aspiring stars. He had been employed as dialogue director for David Selznick on the producer's Technicolor opus, *The Garden of Allah*. Both Fonda and Stewart offered him open house when he arrived. No need to find digs – just shack up with them. Logan gratefully accepted, but after a few days he sensed that both men were somewhat removed from those he had known when all three had worked together in New York. The heady atmosphere of Hollywood had got to them and he didn't like it.

He recalled somewhat waspishly: 'When I'd been there a little while, we all went off to a party at Ginger Rogers' house with whom Stewart was involved at the time. We started to have arguments on the way. I thought both of them had changed. We got into a difference of opinion about Max Reinhardt's Shakespeare film *A Midsummer Night's Dream* which I liked.'

'I saw it and it stinks,' said Jimmy.

'How can you say that? It's a work of art.'

'It won't make a nickel.'

'How could you change so quickly from a man of ideals? You sound like a crass distributor who can think only in picture grosses.'

'That's the way they judge films out here and anyway it stinks.'

Logan continued: 'I got more and more drunk at the party. Fonda and Stewart cornered me and told me they didn't like the way I was behaving. I said: 'Well, I don't like the way Mr James "Hollywood" Stewart was talking to me. I think you've all sold out for money. I'm gonna move out of your money-tainted house. You go your way and I'll go mine.' So saying, he went although the row was short lived and it wasn't long before the three men were back together at Brentwood along with another University Playhouse veteran Johnny Swope.

By the end of his first year at Metro Stewart had got through a phenomenal nine movies. He'd played two newspapermen (*Murder Man, Next Time We Love*), two killers (*Rose Marie, After The Thin Man*), two All-American boys (*Wife vs. Secretary, Small Town Girl*), a romantic aristocrat (*The Gorgeous Hussy*), a racing car driver (*Speed*), even a singing naval officer (*Born To Dance*). All of which was pretty good going by any yardstick. It didn't equal the achievement of Clark Gable who in 1931 had appeared in no fewer than eleven films and by the year's end finished up a star, but it was a record of which Stewart was reasonably proud.

His one nagging worry was that Metro didn't seem to know what to do with him. He wasn't a matinée idol type like Robert Taylor who had joined the studio just a year before Stewart and because of his fine physique and masculine beauty, had risen more quickly. If anything he was more in the Gary Cooper mould and he winced at Alistair Cooke's summing up of his performance in *Born To Dance*: 'There is James Stewart trying to be ingenuous and charming like Gary Cooper but many tricks and years behind.' His singing of Cole Porter's 'Easy to Love' had been embarrassing enough in that picture. To have his acting criticized as well was adding insult to injury.

What it really came down to was that Metro couldn't make up their minds whether he was a light comedian or a romantic leading man. That he might be something different, a genuine original, a 'Jimmy Stewart', didn't seem to enter their thinking. Instead they tried photographing him outdoors, leaning over fences, working with a shovel, holding a tennis racket, to see if it would help promote an outdoor image such as the one enjoyed by Taylor, but it didn't work.

Ted Allan was one of the studio's leading portrait photographers of the time. He had the job of photographing Stewart for publicity purposes. He summed it up when he said: 'There was no problem in making him look handsome – he had great eyes and a generous mouth, but in the time I worked with him I wouldn't have guessed that he'd become a star.'

As if to prove that they were indeed at a loss as to what to do with him, MGM even tested him for the role of Ching in Pearl Buck's saga of Chinese peasant life, *The Good Earth*. The idea was patently ridiculous. Not surprisingly, Stewart remembered it well:

The make up took all morning. They put a bald cap on my head, yanked up my eyelids with spirit gum and trimmed my eyelashes. That was bad enough but in any case I was too tall. They had to dig a trench which I walked in as I trudged alongside the film's star Paul Muni. Then he started to lose his balance and on one occasion tripped and fell headlong into the ditch. After three days of testing Mayer called a halt. I didn't get the part. They gave it to a little Chinese fella.

3 The Blade of Beverly Hills

Mayer doesn't know what he's got. He'll
come round. You'll see.
Leland Hayward

'The eternal innocent', was how one critic described James
Stewart's screen persona. 'He's the boy next door whose
bashful stammers charm virgins into true love – not beds.'
This was the verdict delivered after Stewart had been
eighteen months at Metro. In real life he seemed very
much the same as he did on screen: innocent, gawky,
attractive – and available, all of which made him good
copy for the gossip columnists. 'This one's available and
the Hollywood ladies are standing in line', was the general
tone of their features.

Colliers referred to him as 'The Blade Of Beverly Hills'.
They saw him as a man with a different kind of appeal
than that of Valentino or Gable or Robert Taylor. They
wrote: 'He has an alert, kiddish, eagle-beaked appearance
and everybody likes him. He is the kid from Elm Street
who rents his tux to go to the junior prom. There is no
telling how he will end up in movies. The audiences seem
to like him and the movie lasses draw straws to see who
will be the next lady of the evening. One noted Hollywood
person could see no mystery in his appeal: 'It's simple
enough. A big, goodnatured kid like that, they like to
mother him.'

One who certainly wanted to do rather more than that
was Norma Shearer. The first lady of MGM, she had
recently been widowed by the death of Metro's
production chief Irving Thalberg. She wasted no time in
making a quick swathe through some of Hollywood's

youngest stars. The 16-year-old Mickey Rooney, twenty years her junior, was one. Stewart, six years younger, was another. They met at a costume party held by Marion Davies. Josh Logan was also among the guests. He said:

> Jimmy was being skittish about the lavish attentions of the studio queen. In a moment of alcoholic gallantry he told Shearer, with blazing eyes, that she was the most gorgeous creature he had ever seen. Jimmy's remark hit her like a thunderbolt, which was more than he reckoned on.
>
> Afterwards, she took royal possession of him. She transported him around town openly in her yellow limousine, even though he slumped down on the back seat hoping that his friends would not recognise him.
>
> As proof of her 'ownership' she gave him a gold cigarette case sprinkled with diamonds. That meant that whenever she asked for a cigarette in front of others, the gift would advertise the giver. Jimmy didn't want any sly looks. He would fumble in every pocket until he came up with a crumpled pack of Lucky Strikes. It was his badge as a free man![1]

It took a bit of doing but Stewart eventually escaped the clutches of the possessive and over-eager Shearer. He made it clear that he was not interested in getting involved with anyone and would much prefer to carry on his bachelor existence in Brentwood, along with Hank Fonda and Johnny Swope. In the end Shearer took the hint and let him go.

The Brentwood group was a close-knit community made up largely of New Yorkers who had moved to California to try their hands at the movies. Agent Leland Hayward and his actress wife Margaret Sullavan were at the centre of things. They lived on Evanston Street, a long charming street given additional splendour by the surrounding fields of Avocado trees. Their house was a perpetual hive of activity mainly because most of their friends were also Hayward's clients. Stewart and Swope were frequent visitors as was Hank Fonda, newly married to the beautiful young divorcee Frances Seymour Brokaw. Martha and Roger Edens were always dropping by. Josh Logan was another regular. So too were the

Herman Mankiewiczs. It was a very select little clan.

It was from Hayward that Stewart learned about the 'other side' of Hollywood, the intrigues that went on behind the cameras, the wheeling and dealing that took place in the offices of the movie moguls. Known as a 'high-class gent' Hayward was a tall, thin, distinguished looking man. He had begun in the business by inventing stories for fan magazines and then continued as a press agent, a talent scout and general contact man for studios in New York and Hollywood. He became a full-time agent when he sold a manuscript written by his friend Ben Hecht to MGM. His first star client was Fred Astaire.

By the time Stewart got to know him his 'stable' had grown to impressive proportions. Garbo, Hemingway, Ginger Rogers, Myrna Loy, Fredric March, Edna Ferber, Boris Karloff, Charles Laughton, Helen Hayes, Lillian Hellman were just some of his clients. He knew Hollywood inside out and was generally considered to be the best agent in town. His method of closing a deal was well known. He referred to it often:

It works like this. You call the executives of five or six studios – Warners, Columbia, Paramount, MGM, RKO. You sound excited. Then you tell them that they should check the box-office receipts and the reviews of some plays that have opened in New York, having made sure that you have arranged to handle the motion picture sales of these just an hour before.

Then, having charged up the atmosphere, you leave the office before they can call back. You have a relaxed lunch with a client at the Brown Derby and then maybe do an hour or two's leisurely shopping. By the time you get back to the office there will be twenty hysterical phone calls waiting from the studios, all of them bidding against one another. You then close the deal calmly for a record price.'[2]

Hayward was similarly astute when bargaining for his clients. Often he would use the insult technique. He would settle one haunch on the corner of a mogul's desk and say: 'Jack, why don't you stop cheating the public and actually do a *good* picture for a change instead of just talking about it. Now I happen to have a writer ... and for the leading role an actor who would be just right ...'

To Stewart he was a Godsend! Stewart's friendship with Hayward blossomed not only on an agent-client basis, but also because both men had an obsession with flying. Stewart's had begun way back when he was in his early teens and the barnstormers had visited his home town with their dare-devil acrobatics and flying displays. One of the great moments of his boyhood was when, having saved up fifteen dollars, he had been allowed by his father to go up for twenty minutes and get a taste of what it was like to fly through the clouds.

The bug never left him. A plane of his own was his ambition. Urged on by Hayward, he learned to fly and bought himself a two-seater Stinson I05. Together, agent and actor would spend many contented hours soaring across the cloudless blue skies above Hollywood. Their favourite time of day was dawn, before they faced up to the rigours of life in a studio or an agent's office on Wilshire Boulevard. Given the chance, both men would have stayed aloft all day.

With his audacious manner and ability to take on the studio bosses, Hayward was the perfect agent for Stewart in the late thirties. When the actor confessed that he still enjoyed working at MGM, but didn't seem to be getting anywhere, Hayward told him to wait for the loan-outs. If Metro didn't know what to do with him the loan-outs would be sure to follow. It was then that the studio would make up their minds. 'It's the best thing that can happen Jimmy,' he said. 'Mayer doesn't know what he's got. He'll come round. You'll see.'

Hayward was quickly proved right. At RKO director George Stevens asked for Stewart's services for his comedy, *Vivacious Lady*. Stewart played a young botany professor and Ginger Rogers the nightclub singer with whom he falls in love. The result was one of the best comedy films of the year. Next came Frank Capra. He was filming *You Can't Take It With You* at his home studio of Columbia. Stewart joined an all-star cast that included Jean Arthur, Lionel Barrymore, Edward Arnold, Ann Miller and Spring Byington.

A Pulitzer Prize-winning play, *You Can't Take It With You*

stemmed from the pens of George S. Kaufman and Moss Hart. It centred on the eccentric Vanderhof family, the head of which had given up work some twenty-five years earlier to enjoy life and encourage others to do the same. At loggerheads with the Vanderhofs is a banker, a grasping tycoon who heads one of the largest individual monopolies in the world. He wants to reduce the Vanderhof home to rubble so that he can build still more factories on the vacant site. The two people who eventually bring the families together are Jean Arthur, just about the only sane member of the Vanderhof clan, and Stewart as the shy sensitive son of the tycoon.

Stewart's romancing of Arthur leads to many of the film's most delightful moments, notably a brilliantly comic scene in a nightclub. A wide-eyed Stewart tells Arthur that every time he thinks how lucky he is he feels like screaming and that he can feel a scream coming on right at that moment. Arthur looks aghast:

'You're not going to … ' she begins.

'Yeah,' he replies. 'I can feel it rising, it's coming up, it's in my stomach. Now it's in my chest. It's reached my throat …'

So absorbed has Arthur become that it is she who eventually screams causing Stewart to hide his face in embarrassment as the hubbub in the crowded restaurant is stilled. It remains a wonderfully well-timed and well-played sequence – a tribute not only to the skill of the two performers but also to Capra.

Capra was altogether a new experience for Stewart. At MGM he had been guided by a series of talented professional directors, men like Clarence Brown, Sam Wood, W.S. Van Dyke. They knew their trade, how to make a polished piece of entertainment and how to bring it in on time. All were accomplished craftsmen, but all were interchangeable. If one was suddenly called off a picture to work on another project someone else would be brought in to shoot the final scenes. No-one would notice the difference.

With Capra things were different. At little Columbia he was the boss. His pictures were *his* pictures. No one else ever tampered with them. It was part of the agreement he had with Columbia's tough, crude-talking boss Harry Cohn. When Capra had first joined the studio as a gag writer in the mid-twenties, Columbia was a barely respectable outfit. Its movies were mostly second rate, its stars usually those who had known better days at bigger studios and who were on the way down. Known initially as CBC it had earned the unenviable nickname of 'Corned Beef and Cabbage'. Capra's movies, many of them sentimental comedies with a message, had helped transform it from a laughing stock into a major studio. Harry Cohn, recognizing his young director's skill and youthful enthusiasm, had given him his head and Capra had delivered. *Lady for a Day, It Happened One Night, Mr Deeds Goes to Town,* and *Lost Horizon,* had all swelled the Columbia coffers in the thirties.

You Can't Take It With You belonged in the same mould as many of Capra's earlier works. Basically a comedy that at times bordered on farce, it was also a serious indictment of man valuing money and material possessions rather than his love for his fellow man. It won Capra his third Academy Award in just five years making him the first director to be honoured on three occasions.

It was the first Academy Award winning picture Stewart had appeared in and he enjoyed the feeling. Columbia, with its handful of sound stages was minute when compared with Metro or Paramount yet his weeks with Capra on *You Can't Take It With You* had been the most enjoyable of his entire career. Capra had cheered him by telling him that he was sure they would work together again.

In the meantime MGM welcomed him back by announcing that they had the perfect picture for him. They put him on ice with Joan Crawford in *Ice Follies of 1939.* The result was a disaster. For the first time since he'd started at MGM Stewart began to wonder just what he was doing there.

Footnotes

1. *Josh: My Up and Down, In and Out Life,* Joshua Logan, Delacorte Press (1976)
2. *Haywire,* Brooke Hayward, Alfred A. Knopf (1977)

4 Mr Smith and Mr Destry

'He looked like the country kid, the
idealist. It was very close to him.'
Frank Capra

James Stewart was a long way from Frank Capra's
thoughts when the director walked into Harry Cohn's
office to discuss his next project. He was fired up. 'Harry, I
want to make a film about the life of Chopin.'

Cohn's reaction was predictable.

'What the fucking hell for?' he growled.

Capra ignored the response and went into his pitch.

'It'll be great Harry. It'll be a big picture, bigger than
anything Columbia's ever done. Bigger than *Lost Horizon*.
Think of the prestige, think of the Oscars ... '

He paused to let the last point sink in and then he
continued.

'We need a big cast, plenty of stars. I'm not sure about
the lead but Dietrich would be perfect for George Sand.
I'm sure we can get her.'

'*Anyone* can get her,' snapped Cohn. 'Paramount let her
go last year. She's box-office poison. You know that as
well as I do.'

'That won't matter,' said Capra. 'The story and the
music will carry it. And what's more we'll have
Technicolor.'

Cohn nearly slipped off his chair.

'T-E-C-H-N-I-C-O-L-O-R!'

'Yeah, I know it's expensive, but everyone's using it
now. We've got to use it. It's the future Harry. We can't
miss. Think of it.'

Cohn did think of it. And he reckoned they most

certainly could miss. Warners had just milked dry the biographical cycle of the thirties. The public seemed tired of them. What is more, costume dramas and historical subjects were expensive to produce and the profit margins were small. That's why they tried to stay away from them at Columbia. In any case costume dramas confused him. He'd once torn a writer apart over a script for a Columbia picture. It had been one of the rare occasions that he had ventured into a period setting and the occasion was marked indelibly on his mind. 'Don't you know how people talked in those days?' he roared at the luckless writer. 'This script is full of people saying "siree". Haven't you done *any* research?' Nervously, the writer pointed out that the word was "sire" and that it was the correct form of address.

Capra's enthusiasm for *The Life of Chopin* put Cohn in an awkward position. Capra was his top director. He had been with him throughout the thirties. Without him Columbia would not have survived. Cohn both admired and respected him, but there was no doubt that the proposed movie was a very un-Columbia like project. As a gesture Cohn put the idea to the head office in New York. The response was as he had expected -- no dice. 'Forget it Frank', said Cohn. 'Find something else. How about another *Mr Deeds Goes to Town*. That would be great.'

'I've made Mr Deeds', snapped Capra, smarting from the rebuff and retreating into a funk. 'If I can't make Chopin I won't make anything.'

He stormed back to his office and fumed at his secretary. 'Pack my things, clear my desk. I'm finished with Columbia.' He was still smarting when writer Sam Briskin put his head round the door. He'd heard about the row. In his hand he held a two-page outline of a story called 'The Man From Montana'. He waved it cheerfully. 'Seen this Frank? Might be right up your alley.'

'Nothing's up my alley,' said Capra, snatching the pages from Briskin. 'I'm leaving this goddamned place.' A few minutes later his secretary was putting things back on his desk. 'You're right Sam. This is better than *Mr Deeds*. Get me Cooper. Get me Riskin. This is it.' The story that so excited him was about an idealistic young senator who is chosen to represent his state when the incumbent representative dies. He exposes graft, corruption and skulduggery among his fellow senators and in a determined effort to prevent a bill going through, rouses the nation with a twenty-three-hour filibuster. Honesty and goodwill prevail and win the day. Mr Smith is declared a hero.

For Capra the story was a gift from heaven. He'd always had an affinity with tales that sided with the common man fighting corruption in high places. Many times during the thirties he said: 'I want to glorify the average man, not the guy at the top, not the politicians, not the banker. Just the ordinary guy whose strength I admire, whose survivability I admire.'

The new story fitted the bill perfectly. Here was his chance to go for the jugular of American politics. The theme was controversial – it could be dynamite. Chopin was forgotten. This time Harry Cohn did not stand in his way. He didn't even talk with the head office. 'Go ahead,' he said happy that *The Life of Chopin* had been laid to rest. Capra retitled the story *Mr Smith Goes to Washington* and set about casting.

James Stewart came into the scheme of things because Capra had been impressed with him during the making of *You Can't Take It With You* and because he was younger than the other candidate for the leading role, Gary Cooper. It had always been touch and go as to which of the two actors would play Mr Smith. At first, Capra favoured Cooper. He had been superb as the tuba-playing country boy in *Mr Deeds Goes to Town*. Capra was anxious to work with him again, but Stewart had the edge. 'Jim was younger,' said Capra. 'I knew he would make a hell of a Mr Smith. He looked like the country kid, the idealist. It was very close to him. I think there's no doubt that this picture shaped the public image of him, of the real Jimmy Stewart.'

Stewart himself could hardly believe his luck. It was all too obvious that MGM were still unsure of what to do with him yet here was the most successful director in Hollywood offering him one of the plum roles of the year. In April, 1939, he found himself driving through the gates of little Columbia for the second time within a year. The irony of the situation was not lost on him. The biggest studio in Hollywood could find no way of using him; one of the smallest was offering him a part that most actors would have given their eye-teeth for.

Stewart became so caught up in the filming of *Mr Smith Goes to Washington* that he even agreed to see the rushes. He'd always avoided them at Metro but Capra's house was in the same direction as Stewart's. When the director offered him a lift home and, along the way, a chance to see the rushes in his own private projection room, Stewart was flattered. He agreed to break his long standing rule, but quickly found out that it was a mistake. He discovered that a perfectionist like Capra looked at rushes and rushes, and yet more rushes. Stewart said:

> The first time I stopped off at Capra's house I was there an hour and forty minutes. There was take after take, from every angle. He really covered himself. Every scene from every angle. Well, I didn't stay to the end.
>
> The next night it was clearly going to be even longer! After an hour I turned to Frank. He was fast asleep. Well, I didn't wake him or anything. I waited through the whole thing, but at last I said: 'Frank, I got sort of against rushes at Metro. If it's all right with you I don't think I want to see anymore.'

The key moment in *Mr Smith*, and the most difficult, was the long filibuster sequence in which Stewart makes his impassioned plea for honesty and tolerance. It took over a week to film and Capra covered the scene with six cameras as Stewart set about exposing the corruption in the senate. Superb throughout the sequence, he was especially fine in the final minutes as he gasps in a hoarse voice: 'You think I'm licked. Well, I'm not licked. I'm going to stay right here and fight for this lost cause. Somebody will listen to me.' Unable to stand after twenty-three hours on his feet he collapses in a faint.

The main problem for Stewart was not so much the acting which was strenuous enough, but to get the right sound to his voice. He had been practising as to how best he could sound hoarse. In the end he came up with a kind of rasp. Capra was unimpressed. He said bluntly: 'All that sounds like is an actor trying to put on a voice with a rasp.' Stewart immediately became worried as to whether he could pull it off. On the way home he stopped off at an eye, ear, nose and throat doctor and asked him if there was anything he could give him that would make his throat sore. Stewart said:

The doctor was kinda surprised. He shook his head and then said 'I've heard you Hollywood folk are kinda crazy, but you take the cake. You want me to give you a sore throat. It's taken me twenty-five years of study and practice to keep people from getting sore throats. Now you want me to give you one.'

He wasn't happy about it, but after a lot of muttering he said: 'OK, I'll give you the sorest throat you've ever had.'

He dropped dichloride of mercury into my throat, not near my vocal chords, but just in around there. It wasn't dangerous. And he said: 'how's that?' I said: 'rasp, rasp'. He said: 'You got it.'

The doctor actually came onto the set to keep me under supervision in case the effects of the mercury should wear off. I was afraid Capra would say something about my becoming a mechanical actor, but he didn't mind. He said it was fine.

So indeed did most of the critics when *Mr Smith Goes to Washington* was premièred. The picture met with some hostility in Washington where many were angered that corruption should be implied to exist in the capital. There were even walk outs at a special showing for senators and press officials. In New York and elsewhere across the country, however, there was nothing but praise for both the film and for Stewart's performance. *Newsweek* was unstinting in its praise: 'With the exception of a few sorties into the extra-callow James Stewart gives the most persuasive characterisation of his career as a home-made crusader against political corruption.' *The Nation* was also quick to hand out plaudits:

> *Mr Smith Goes to Washington* is by far and away the best
> Hollywood picture of the year. James Stewart as Jefferson
> Smith takes first place among Hollywood actors … Now he
> is mature and gives a difficult part, with many nuances,
> moments of tragi-comic impact. And he is able to do more
> than play isolated scenes effectively. He shows the growth
> of a character through experience. In the end he is so
> forceful that his victory is thoroughly credible.

While all this euphoria was taking place Stewart was
filming the final scenes on yet another loan-out picture,
Destry Rides Again. It was his first western, a comedy spoof
about a peace loving marshal who tames a Wild West
town without the use of guns. It had been filmed once
before as a Tom Mix western back in 1932. New characters
had been added for the remake, among them Frenchy, the
dance-hall hostess who falls for the young lawman and
stops a bullet in saving his life.

This time the studio was Universal which, if anything,
had been in even more trouble than Columbia in the
thirties and had been saved from bankruptcy only by the
horror films of Karloff and Lugosi and the sweet
disposition and singing voice of Deanna Durbin. The
producer of the Durbin musicals was Joe Pasternak.
Because of the success of the Durbin films he had earned
himself a position of some power at the studio. So when
he proposed making a western the Universal bosses had
no hesitation in going along with the idea, especially as
the genre, through such pictures as Cecil B. DeMille's
Union Pacific and *The Plainsman*, had shown signs of
making a comeback.

When Pasternak suggested that Marlene Dietrich would
be ideal for the role of the saloon singer Frenchy, however,
their reaction was very much the same as that of Harry
Cohn when Capra had mentioned her for George Sand in
his *Life of Chopin*. They tried gently to persuade Pasternak
from casting her. Out came the same arguments:
box-office poison, washed-up, a has-been, no longer a
draw. How about Hedy Lamarr or Paulette Goddard?
Pasternak didn't want Hedy Lamarr. Neither did he want
Goddard. He wanted Dietrich, plus the young Jimmy

Stewart as Destry. He sensed that together they would make an unusual and potent box-office team. He refused to be swayed.

Reluctantly Universal agreed and Pasternak went ahead and contacted Dietrich. She was then living in the south of France. Her reaction was hostile: 'Not for anything in the world.' Her mentor, director Josef von Sternberg who had himself hit hard times quicker than he had expected, advised her to accept. She cabled Pasternak that she was on her way to Hollywood.

When she arrived Pasternak found that he still needed all his powers of persuasion. She would read the script, she said. *Then* she would decide. Otherwise, it was back to France. In reality she was in no position to bargain. She needed the money. She accepted at a salary of $75,000, just a sixth of what she had been earning at Paramount. She was no longer the impeccably dressed sophisticate of such films as *Desire* and Ernst Lubitsch's *Angel*. Instead, she was a tousled haired bar-room entertainer, a full-blooded woman who fought tooth and nail for what she wanted.

As an extra piece of persuasion Pasternak hired her favourite composer Frederick Hollander. He had written 'Falling in Love Again' for *The Blue Angel*. He hit the mark again in *Destry* with a song that was to become one of Dietrich's trademarks: 'See What the Boys in the Back-Room Will Have.' To her surprise Dietrich enjoyed filming *Destry Rides Again*. The atmosphere was easy-going and pleasant. There were no hassles as there had been on the expensive productions at Paramount. Also, she enjoyed learning things for her part such as making her own cigarettes western style and using her teeth to open the neck of the sack of wet tobacco. Most of all she enjoyed James Stewart. Pasternak said:

> She took one look at Jimmy Stewart and began to rub her hands. She wanted him at once. He was just a nice, simple guy who loved Flash Gordon comics. That was all he seemed to read on set.
>
> I remember she did something incredible. When he was in his dressing room she locked the door and wouldn't let him out. But she promised that she would come back with

a surprise. The surprise was a doll, a life-size doll of Flash Gordon. She had persuaded the art department to come in over the weekend and make it up for him. It was correct in every detail. It started a short romance.[1]

The big moment in *Destry* was a no-holds-barred fight between Dietrich and Una Merkel, a townswoman who accuses Dietrich of stealing her husband. Stewart participated in the scene, but only briefly at the end of the scrap. He needed none of the sweat and tears of his filibuster scene in *Mr Smith Goes to Washington*. Just a few words and a pail of water, tipped over the girls as he brings the fight to a close.

Everyone enjoyed the fight in *Destry*, not least the two actresses involved. Many, and Stewart was among them, were surprised that Dietrich entered so wholeheartedly into the thing. Director George Marshall gave them no special instructions. He just said: 'Let it rip,' which is what they did. Una Merkel said:

Neither of us knew what we were doing. We just plunged in and punched and slapped and kicked for all we were worth. They never did call in the stunt girls. Marlene stepped on my feet with her French heels. The toenails *never* grew back. She was stronger than me. She was very powerful and I was very thin. Luckily, I have a remarkable constitution. I was bruised from head to foot when it was over. I looked like an old peach, green with brown spots. And I felt like one too.

At the end of the scene Jimmy Stewart came in and dumped a whole bucket of water over us. He did it in long shot. Then he had to do it over for close-ups. Then *Life* Magazine wanted pictures so they did it over again. He dumped water on us for hours.[2]

For Stewart, *Destry Rides Again* was a relatively easy film to make, something of a battery recharger after the rigours of *Mr Smith Goes to Washington*, but he enjoyed his first venture West and regarded the film as a piece of luck. He said:

My dad had taught me to ride a horse when I was a kid so I was all right in that department. And as I was just a contract player at Metro it was good to be considered for the role.

The only complaints I got were from western picture buffs across the country. They weren't very complimentary about it because they felt that I didn't present the western sheriff in the right light. He should have been tougher I guess. That's how they felt anyhow. But other than that the reaction was good.

In her autobiography Dietrich made no mention of her romance with Stewart, but she did recall him with a kind of affectionate mockery. She wrote:

He belonged to the 'whatever happened to my other shoe' period. Jimmy Stewart was the original inventor of this style. Even when he made a visible effort to play a love scene he always gave the impression he was wearing only one shoe and looking for the other one while he slowly droned his lines. One day I told him about these ruminations of mine and he answered: 'How's that?' He performed this way throughout his life and became very rich and very famous. Now he no longer has to look for his other shoe.[3]

Destry Rides Again was a boisterous, amusing and different kind of western that didn't take itself too seriously. It was well received critically, but didn't make it into the ten best films of the year because 1939 was a year like no other in the history of movies. By a fluke, just about all the major film-makers in Hollywood came up with some of their best efforts: John Ford made *Stagecoach* and *Young Mr Lincoln*; William Wyler filmed *Wuthering Heights*; in England Sam Wood directed *Goodbye Mr Chips*; Lubitsch hit top form with *Ninotchka*; George Stevens filmed the best adventure romp of the decade, *Gunga Din*; William Dieterle put Charles Laughton through torturous makeup in *The Hunchback of Notre Dame*; and topping them all was David Selznick's version of *Gone With the Wind*.

Never before and never since had critics had so much difficulty in selecting 'the best' of the year. No matter which category they concentrated on there were always at least half-a-dozen candidates up for consideration.

In December 1939, the New York critics spent hour after hour deliberating. In the end they went to fourteen ballots in trying to decide which film was the best of the year – *Gone With the Wind* or *Mr Smith Goes to Washington*? In the end, unable to decide and needing sleep, food and sustenance to keep them going they decided on a compromise – *Wuthering Heights*, a decision which in retrospect seems not a little baffling. The obvious solution would have been to have split the vote and name both as best of the year, but no such thoughts occurred. *Wuthering Heights* emerged as the winner.

For best actor though they were much more clear cut in their choice. On the third ballot Stewart emerged ahead of Robert Donat (*Goodbye Mr Chips*) and Henry Fonda (*Young Mr Lincoln*) as the year's top male performer. It was an award that put Stewart in line for the biggest prize of all, the one Frank Capra kept referring to as the 'Holy Grail' of the movie business – the Oscar! It was a prize that during his five years in Hollywood Stewart had never once considered to be within his reach. Now, thanks to Metro having loaned him out to other studios, especially Columbia, he knew that it was.

Footnotes

1. *Marlene*, Charles Higham, Granada Publishing (1978)
2. *Ibid.*
3. *Marlene Dietrich: My Life*, Weidenfeld & Nicolson (1989)

5   The Philadelphia Story

'The reason Jimmy stood out from other actors was that he had the ability to talk naturally.'

Cary Grant

The gossip in Hollywood in the early weeks of 1940 was that Stewart was favourite for the Oscar and that *Mr Smith* might even steal the best picture award from *Gone With the Wind*. When the nominations were announced, rumour became fact. *Gone With the Wind* received thirteen, and *Mr Smith* was close behind with ten including nods for best picture, best director and best actor.

Stewart himself didn't give too much credence to the rumours or indeed the nominations. He preferred to keep a low profile, although that often proved difficult with friends constantly reminding him that he was in with an excellent chance. Hank Fonda, who rather unluckily hadn't made the nominations for *Young Mr Lincoln*, assured him that people were talking of him as a likely winner. Capra too made reassuring noises: 'I've been to a lot of these things Jimmy. We've all got a great chance. The New York Critics Award will help. It always does. Sure the competition is tough, but then it is every year.'

Stewart kept his own counsel. Four words kept coming into his mind: *Gone With the Wind*. Harry Cohn, however, was another who refused to be daunted, pulling out all the stops, spending money to promote the film and getting publicity where it really counted, from the influential gossip columnists. Sheila Graham left no one in any doubt as to what she thought of *Mr Smith* calling it 'the best talking picture ever made.' Hedda Hopper also favoured excessive hyperbole: 'To me Frank Capra's film is as great as Lincoln's Gettysburg speech.' The icing on the cake was provided by the then popular film magazine *Screen Book* which predicted that *Mr Smith Goes to Washington* would win *every* Academy Award.'

As things turned out Stewart was right to harbour doubts. Not for the first time the West Coast disagreed with New York. The competition did indeed prove too tough. Frank Capra had been unduly optimistic. He was more disappointed than anyone. He later commented: 'We were unlucky … our film got bounced around in *Gone With the Wind*'s slipsteam.'

From its ten nominations *Mr Smith* picked up just one award, for best original story, which went to writer Lewis R. Foster. The rest, including Stewart, finished nowhere. Only Robert Donat, best actor for his ageing schoolmaster in *Goodbye Mr Chips* and Thomas Mitchell, best supporting actor for *Stagecoach*, prevented a *Gone With the Wind* whitewash. The film picked up nine awards, dominating the evening from first to last.

For those not associated with *Gone With the Wind* the evening was not only a disappointment, but also an anti-climax. The *Los Angeles Times*, which had been sworn to secrecy, broke their agreement with the Academy and published a full list of the winners in their 8.45 edition. Those arriving late for the banquet at the Ambassador Hotel's Cocoanut Grove were thus able to read who had won and who had lost before their sleek limousines pulled up outside the hotel. An evening that was usually tinged with excitement and full of surprises fell unexpectedly flat.

One who had the embarrassment of having to remain seated throughout the three-hour ceremony was Clark Gable. He was one of the few *Gone With the Wind* nominees who did not receive a statuette. If Stewart was philosophical in defeat, Gable was angry. He'd already been a winner once in the thirties for Capra's *It Happened One Night* and would have given much to have joined his MGM buddy Spencer Tracy as the only double best actor winner of the decade. Mrs Gable (actress Carole Lombard) did her best to raise his spirits on the way home: 'Aw, don't be blue Pappy, I just know we'll bring one home next year.'

'No we won't,' Gable responded. 'This was it. This was my last chance. I'm never going to go to one of those things again.'

'Not you, you self-centred bastard,' replied Lombard. 'I mean me!'

Stewart had no wisecracking wife to help him over his defeat, but as he hadn't really expected to win anyway he didn't let things get to him too much. He took consolation in his New York Critics Award, not as glittery perhaps, but almost as highly prized, and the fact that at last Metro seemed to be taking an interest in him. Apart from loaning him out to Warners for the Rosalind Russell vehicle, *No Time For Comedy*, they kept him at Culver City throughout the year. Admittedly some of their casting seemed a trifle bizarre. Stewart had been nigh on perfect as the idealistic young Mr Smith, but it was straining credulity to its limits to accept him as a Hungarian shop assistant in Lubitsch's delicate comedy *The Shop Around the Corner* and as a Bavarian student fighting the Nazis in Frank Borzage's *The Mortal Storm*. If Stewart had a weakness it was his inability to be totally convincing in a role that was other than that of an American. His languid drawl was ideal for homespun heroes, but something of a hindrance when it came to portraying Europeans. For all that he gave a good account of himself, especially in the Lubitsch picture.

The upside of both movies was that they teamed him with his long-time friend Margaret Sullavan. They had already worked together twice before on screen: at Universal in 1936 in the mawkish soap opera *Next Time We Love* and at Metro two years later in *The Shopworn Angel*, another romantic tale about the love affair between a stage actress and a young soldier in World War I. On both occasions Sullavan had played Stewart's love interest. It was the same with the two new movies. *The Shop Around the Corner* was about two quarrelsome shop assistants who unknown to themselves carry on an affectionate correspondence as pen friends, and *The Mortal Storm* had Sullavan as the daughter of a university professor who dies in Stewart's arms just as they reach the border and safety.

Working with Sullavan was one of the great joys for Stewart in the late thirties. He knew her moods, understood her temperament and could handle any sudden emotional crisis that might occur on set. Which is more than could be said for many who found themselves embroiled in a Sullavan picture. Unlike Stewart they did not have the advantage of knowing her personally. They found her moments of temper and unpredictability hard to take.

One who had a particularly hard time of it was William Wyler, one of her three husbands of the thirties. During the shooting of *The Good Fairy* at Universal she was difficult, unco-operative and just plain impossible. When he would suggest one way of doing a scene she would do the opposite; when he tried to guide her through an especially awkward part of the script she would refuse to listen. Wyler suffered most of her tantrums in silence. Then one day he blew! In front of the whole crew he told her:

> Now you listen and don't interrupt. You've made work on this picture last for twelve weeks instead of seven and you've all but demoralized me. This is the end. You're going to enter left, stand on that chalk mark, and twist that vicious pan of yours into the semblance of a human face and drench this scene with pathos. And you're not going to underplay or suffer silently by gritting your teeth. And then you're going to cry – get it? Bawl! And like it!'

Sullavan walked off the set. For Stewart, Sullavan was more beguiling than temperamental. He found it difficult to remain angry with her for long because after an outburst she would be radiant and vivacious and full of warmth and laughter. He was also very susceptible to her charms, but there were times when even he found it difficult to fathom her moods and her acting technique. He said:

> When you played a scene with her you were never sure, although she was letter perfect, what was going to happen. She had you just a little bit off guard and also the director ... she could do moments that would hit you, maybe a look or a line or two, but they would hit like flashes or earthquakes, everybody would sort of feel it at the same

time. She hated talk. Lots of times she'd say: 'We're talking too much, we don't need all this talk.' She would never sit around and discuss a scene.'[1]

During a relatively simple scene in *The Shop Around the Corner* Stewart experienced the full brunt of Sullavan's impatience. One line was the cause of all the trouble. It took forty-eight takes to get it right. It was the most takes Stewart ever did in the movies. He said:

We were in this little restaurant and I had the line: 'I will come out on the street and I will roll my trousers up to my knees.' For some reason I couldn't say it. She was furious. She said: 'This is absolutely ridiculous.'

There I was, standing with my trousers rolled up to my knees, very conscious of my skinny legs, and I said: 'I don't want to act today; get a fellow with decent legs and just show them.' Margaret said: 'Then I absolutely refuse to do the picture.' So we did more takes.[2]

The Shop Around the Corner and *The Mortal Storm* were the last movies that Stewart and Sullavan made together. For Sullavan they were also the last major pictures of her all-too-brief career in Hollywood. Never a dedicated film actress, she made just a handful of movies in the early forties then returned to the Broadway stage where she achieved considerable success in *The Voice of the Turtle*. Her final picture was *No Sad Songs For Me* made in 1950. She and Stewart remained close friends, however, as did all the Leland Hayward crowd who lived close by in Brentwood.

Off-screen Stewart's romances continued to attract the attention of the Hollywood press. Although many in number they never seemed to amount to very much or last for any great length of time. One that did and looked for a while as though it might be for real was his affair with Olivia de Havilland. The actress entered his life shortly after his brief fling with Dietrich during the filming of *Destry Rides Again*. She was recovering from her well-publicized infatuation with Errol Flynn and an affair with millionaire Howard Hughes. She was struck by Stewart's humble charm and boyish good looks. When they attended the première of *Gone With the Wind* in New York the columnists duly took note.

The typewriters began to click even more furiously when Stewart and de Havilland stayed on in New York enjoying the nightspots, dinner at '21' and attending all the latest Broadway shows. Fan magazines began to run the inevitable headlines: 'Is this it at last for Jimmy Stewart?' It seemed that, for a time at least, he certainly seemed to think so. According to de Havilland he even went so far as to ask her to marry him. She added though that there didn't seem to be much conviction about the proposal. 'He was great fun to be with, a bit like a grown-up Huck Finn,' she said later with affection. 'I think his offer of marriage was just a frivolous thing on his part. Jimmy wasn't ready for a wife. I guess he still had a few more wild oats to sow.'

When the break up eventually came, de Havilland had her eyes set on another long string bean, the director John Huston who had guided her through *In This Our Life* at Warners. Neither she nor Stewart was too broken-hearted about the end of the romance. Stewart commented humorously: 'I just had to stop going out with Olivia de Havilland because I never could say her name properly when I introduced her.'

Stewart's biggest professional break in 1940 occurred when he was offered a role in Metro's film version of Philip Barry's hit play, *The Philadelphia Story*. Katharine Hepburn had starred in the play on Broadway and had shrewdly purchased a percentage of the production costs prior to the opening at the Shubert Theatre. She had also insisted on a clause in her contract that stated that should the play be made into a film she would automatically play the role and that she would also have the choice of her two leading men.

Louis B. Mayer wasn't entirely happy with the situation. He was being forced to take on an actress who, like Dietrich, had been labelled box-office poison. He realized, however, that if he wanted to put the film before the cameras he had no option. Warners had already shown interest and had offered $225,000 for the rights, *without* Hepburn. MGM upped the bid to a quarter of a million and agreed to Hepburn's terms.

The play was about a spoiled heiress, Tracy Lord, who learns humility and a few home truths about herself during the weekend of her proposed second marriage. The wedding is covered by a cynical magazine reporter (with whom the heiress has a brief fling) and his lady photographer. Events are further complicated by the unexpected arrival of the heiress's former husband who subtly baits her, exacerbates her private doubts about the marriage and then woos and weds her for a second time. There was scarcely any plot, just three acts of snappy, witty dialogue that frequently poked mischievous and sometimes malevolent fun at America's leisured classes.

For the roles of the ex-husband and the reporter Hepburn went for the best: Clark Gable and Spencer Tracy. When Mayer informed her that neither was available she agreed to Cary Grant and James Stewart, in retrospect two of the classiest 'replacements' in Hollywood history. Grant had first choice of the two parts. He selected the role of the husband, insisting on top billing and donating all of his $137,500 salary to the British War Relief Fund. Stewart was left with the reporter, on the face of it the least showy of the two parts.

The film was directed by George Cukor, long a favourite of Hepburn's and also no stranger to Grant who had worked with him and Hepburn a couple of years earlier on another Barry comedy, *Holiday*. Stewart found working with the director very nearly as rewarding as filming with Capra. Cukor's touch was lighter, more sophisticated. On set he was patient, quietly spoken and unobtrusive. He was not an improviser, but if something unintentional happened in a scene and it worked he allowed it to stay. Stewart benefited from this in a scene he shared with Grant. The scene required him to be slightly inebriated. Without warning he let out an unscheduled hiccup in the middle of his speech, catching the suave Grant completely off guard. Cukor, enjoying the look of total surprise on Grant's face and his quick attempt to recover, let the scene stand. Grant later remembered:

In that scene I was absolutely fascinated by him. When you watch him you can see how good he is in the film. I think the reason Jimmy stood out from other actors was that he had the ability to talk naturally. He knew that in conversation people *do* often interrupt one another and that it's not always so easy to get a thought out. It took a little while for the sound men to get used to him, but he had an enormous impact. And then, some years later, Marlon Brando came out and did the same thing all over again. But what people forget is that Jimmy did it first. And he affected all of us really.[3]

Director George Stevens who had guided Stewart through *Vivacious Lady*, agreed: 'That's very true when you come to think about it. The difference between Jimmy and Marlon was that Jimmy did it with a kind of emphasis and Brando did it with a kind of reticence.'

Stewart's only real problem on *The Philadelphia Story* occurred when he had to play a scene in which he took the young Hepburn in his arms. Aroused with passion he was required to utter some lines that were, to say the least, flowery and high flown. He found the scene difficult and embarrassing. It had been just a single line that had given him trouble in *The Shop Around the Corner*. In *The Philadelphia Story* it was an entire scene. Katharine Hepburn remembered:

It did really cause him the most terrible distress. He had to say: 'There's a magnificence in you Tracy, a magnificence that comes out of your eyes, that's in your voice, in the way you stand ... You've got fires banked down in you, hearth fires and holocausts.' Well, it was not exactly a Jimmy Stewart line.
Jimmy rehearsed the scene with me and he nearly died. George Cukor said: 'Jimmy, you're not running away to the circus so don't paw the ground with your foot. Just *say* it.' And Jimmy took a deep breath and he said it. He was magnificent.[4]

Cukor put *The Philadelphia Story* before the cameras on 3 July 1940 and brought it in five days under schedule on 14 August. The première was at the Radio City Music Hall on

26 December. The critics were almost unanimous in their praise. The only minor criticism was that the pace of the film seemed too leisurely at times. Cukor's defence was that the play (and the film) had serious things to say and dealt with people who said witty things about important things. The slowish pace was because he didn't want laughter drowning out the next funny moment in the movie.

With such good material at his disposal Stewart had anticipated good reviews but he felt that at best he would come in a good third behind Hepburn and Grant. He was surprised therefore when several of the critics, whilst acknowledging that it was Kate Hepburn's movie, singled him out for special praise. Otis Ferguson in *The New Republic* described his performance as 'near perfection' and the critic of *The New York Herald Tribune* wrote warmly: 'Stewart, in the part of the snooping journalist who hates his job and wants to write real stuff, contributes most of the comedy to the show. His reaction to a snobbish society built on wealth is a delight to watch. In addition, he contributes some of the most irresistible romantic moments to the proceedings.'

The film itself was described variously as 'a sophisticated, brittle comedy of manners', 'a witty film of the kind that results naturally and effectively from shrewdly observed characterization' and 'a picture that has the edge of quality champagne, not too sweet, not too light, just the right intoxicating mixture of both.'

Audiences seemed to agree. In its six weeks at the Music Hall the film surprised even MGM by taking nearly $600,000. It also aroused talk of Oscars with the heavy money going on Hepburn for best actress, Cukor for best director and Donald Ogden Stewart for his screenplay. Amid all the feverish predictions no one considered Stewart, and that turned out to be their big mistake.

Footnotes

1. *Haywire*, Brooke Hayward, Alfred A. Knopf (1977)
2. *Ibid.*
3. *Esquire*, Peter Bogdanovich (July 1966)
4. *James Stewart: A Wonderful Life*, Educational Broadcasting Corporation (1987)

6   The Oscar

'Where'd you get that thing? Ocean Park
Pier?'

Burgess Meredith

It was a case of *déjà vu* when the Oscar nominations were
announced in January, 1941. Stewart once again found
himself nominated (for *The Philadelphia Story*) and this time
Hank Fonda also made it into the list of five nominees – for
his Tom Joad in *The Grapes of Wrath*. It was the first time
the two friends had been in direct competition. A week
before the awards Stewart called Fonda to wish him luck.
Fonda laughed it off. 'I ain't worried Jimmy, but thanks
anyway. I was going to ring you tomorrow, just to let you
know I voted for you.'

'Waal, I voted for you Hank. Thought you'd like to
know that.'

'People are saying you could win,' said Fonda.

Stewart didn't think so. 'Can't see it myself. I kinda
reckon I'm the outsider this time. I guess they think I just
play newspapermen pretty well.'

'You goin'?'

'Waal, I don't seem to be able to make up my mind. I'm
pretty bushed. I've got two pictures on the go at Metro
and after all that embarrassment last year ...'

'Well, one thing's for sure. I ain't goin'. I'm getting outa
town.'

Stewart wasn't surprised. Hank Fonda was very
negative about the Academy Awards. 'Where you
headed?'

'Mexico, in Pappy Ford's boat. We're goin' to do some
fishin', get away from it all.'

'Good idea – wish I could join you.'

'You know my views on all the Oscar crap Jimmy – all those movie people in one room. I don't mind the losing bit, it's all those gasps of "not him" if you win.'

'Waal, good luck anyway Hank. And have a good trip.'

About an hour later the telephone rang in Stewart's house. 'Hello, is this Mr James Stewart?'

'Yeah, who is this?'

'Good evening Mr Stewart. You don't know me. I'm from the Academy. I'm checking out the nominees for next week's Oscar banquet. Will you be coming?'

Stewart tried to stall. 'Waal, I am a bit overloaded at the studio right now.'

The man from the Academy sounded disconcerted. 'Well, I do hope you *can* make it Mr Stewart.' He paused as if unsure as to how to continue then added: 'I know it isn't my place to say so but I really think you would find it in your best interests to attend.' With that he hung up.

The call puzzled Stewart. He couldn't make up his mind whether the man really was checking up on all those who would be attending or even if he was from the Academy at all. He hadn't given his name. And even if he was genuine Stewart couldn't believe he knew something. After the débâcle of the previous year the Academy was introducing a sealed envelope system so that no one would know the winners in advance. If the mystery man was from the Academy how was it possible for him to have any prior knowledge of the results?

Nonetheless Stewart was sufficiently intrigued to change his mind and attend the ceremony which had been moved from the Cocoanut Grove to the much larger venue of The Biltmore Hotel. This time, thanks to the sealed envelope, all the tension and excitement was back. The best actor award was one of the last to be announced so it was a long wait and several times during the evening Stewart thought of Hank Fonda and envied him sunning himself on John Ford's boat. The continuing surprises of the night, however, kept making him feel that perhaps he did have an outside chance after all. It was no clean sweep this time. Every film that was nominated seemed to be picking up something: William Wyler's *The Westerner* earned Walter Brennan his third supporting actor award,

The Great McGinty won a writing Oscar for Preston Sturges, Disney's *Pinocchio* received a couple of music awards. *The Thief of Bagdad, Pride and Prejudice, Rebecca, Tin Pan Alley* and *Strike Up the Band* were among the other winners. So too was the much fancied *The Grapes of Wrath* which earned a supporting actress award for Jane Darwell for her Ma Joad and a director's nod for John Ford. It was these two latter awards that made Stewart feel that things would eventually swing Fonda's way.

It fell to Alfred Lunt to read out the list of nominations: 'The nominations for best actor are: Charles Chaplin for *The Great Dictator*' (muted applause, Charlie wasn't too popular); 'Henry Fonda in *The Grapes of Wrath*' (loud applause); 'Raymond Massey in *Abe Lincoln In Illinois*' (polite applause); 'Laurence Olivier in *Rebecca*' (loud applause) 'and' ... Stewart tried to look calm ... 'James Stewart in *The Philadelphia Story*.' Stewart was too tense to notice whether the applause was loud, polite or non-existent. He tried a smile because he knew that everyone was looking at him. Of the five best actor nominees he was the only one who had turned up so perhaps the mystery caller was genuine after all.

Alfred Lunt opened the envelope. 'The winner is ... James Stewart for *The Philadelphia Story*. The applause was thunderous. On a night of surprises this was arguably the biggest surprise of all, and the most popular. As he strode quickly towards the stage Stewart couldn't really believe that he had defeated such quality competition. The applause lasted all the way to the podium. True to his screen image he gulped loudly at the microphone, paused and then said:

> I want to assure you that this is a very, very important moment in my life. As I look around the room, a warm feeling comes over me – a feeling of satisfaction, pride and most of all, gratefulness for the encouragement, instruction and advantage of your experience that has been offered me since I came to Hollywood. With all my heart I thank you.

The Oscar night was doubly enjoyable for James in that his former co-star and romantic companion Ginger Rogers also caused an upset. She won as best actress for her 'girl from the wrong side of the tracks', *Kitty Foyle*. When reporters finally tracked down Katharine Hepburn who made a point of never turning up at the Oscar ceremonies, they asked her what she thought of the result. For many she had been a certain winner for her Tracy Lord. She reacted a trifle haughtily: 'I was offered *Kitty Foyle*, but I didn't want to play a soap opera about a shop girl. Ginger was wonderful. She's enormously talented and deserves the Oscar. As for me, prizes are nothing. My prize is my work.'

After a long and often quite riotous night James eventually managed to find his way back to Brentwood where a mountain of congratulatory messages awaited him, among them an 'I told you so' cable from Hank Fonda. Burgess Meredith who was then staying with him for a few days, brought him down to earth by taking one look at the statuette and commenting: 'Where'd you get that thing – Ocean Park Pier?' James was sobered up even more when his father rang to find out what all the fuss was about. Stewart was scarcely in a fit state for intelligent conversation, but he did his best.

'You won some kind of prize,' said his father. 'I heard it on the radio.'

'Yeah dad. It's a best actor award. They give 'em out every year. I won it for *The Philadelphia Story*. You seen that yet?'

'Never mind about that,' said Stewart senior. 'What kind of prize is it?'

'It's a kind of statuette. Looks like gold but isn't. They call it the Oscar.'

Stewart's father paused for a moment then in a matter-of-fact voice said: 'Well, that's fine I guess. You'd better send it over. I'll put it on show in the store where folks can take a look at it.'

That was just about the extent of his interest. The next day Stewart duly obliged by carefully wrapping the prized statuette and sending it through to Indiana. Within forty-eight hours, the Oscar, coveted by so many, was on show in the family hardware store, its home a glass display case which housed many other curios and mementos collected over the years by the Stewart family, including photographs, medals, and paintings by Stewart's sister.

Once all the hullabaloo had died down Stewart still found it difficult to come to terms with the fact that, at the age of thirty-three, he had become one of the select few to have won Hollywood's most prestigious award. He said later:

> It's funny. I never thought much of my performance in *The Philadelphia Story*. I guess it was slick and smooth and entertaining and all that. But *Mr Smith* had more guts. Many people have suggested that I won it as a kind of deferred payment for my work on *Mr Smith*. I think there's some truth in that because the Academy seems to have a way of paying past debts. But it should have gone to Hank that year. That was one helluva performance he gave for Ford in *The Grapes Of Wrath*.

Despite all the Oscar excitement Stewart's mind was not entirely focused on his acting career in the early weeks of 1941. For the first time since arriving in Hollywood he began to wonder what life might be like if he gave up making movies for a living. For some time he'd been concerned that the United States had not entered the Second World War. The conflict had been raging for eighteen months in Europe and there was still no sign of America coming in to help Britain and what was left of the hard-pressed Allies. Economic assistance, plus weapons, was all that President Roosevelt seemed to be prepared to offer.

Opinion polls showed that most Americans were more anti-war than anti-Nazi. Nonetheless, Stewart, along with several of his close colleagues, was convinced that America's entry was inevitable and he wanted to be ready when it came. His grandfather had fought in the American Civil War, his father in both the Spanish-American War and the First World War. Stewart's ambition was to serve as a pilot in the Air Corps. He had clocked up more than 400 hours in his little two-seat Stinson, but realized that he'd need much more airtime and a lot of training if he was to make it as a pilot. He decided not to wait. Just a few days after winning his Oscar he publicly announced that he would be joining the army as a private.

Louis B. Mayer was stunned by the news. Stewart was now one of his hottest properties. To lose him would be unthinkable. If he did join up others might follow. That would be disastrous for the studio. He decided to act.

Mayer liked to think that he was at his best in times of 'crisis'. His method was to indulge in what he called fatherly chats with his employees. Those on the receiving end of these chats would be told how lucky they were to be working at MGM, how unhappy they would become if they left the studio and that they didn't really need the salary raise they'd asked for when they'd stepped into his office. Mayer invariably won. Stars and directors discovered he could be very persuasive. Most were overawed by his presence. They would leave the office in a daze, totally talked out and defeated. A few days later, sometimes just a few minutes later, they would realize they had been conned, but by then it was too late.

Mayer would even cry if he felt it would help him push home his point. His tears became legendary. Gregory Peck later remarked that he enjoyed it so much he made it a two-performance a day job. On other occasions he would implore a star to take a role by acting out the entire part. Hollywood folklore says he did just that when Greer Garson stalled about taking on *Mrs Miniver*. None of this was any use, of course, in Stewart's case. Studio problems weren't the issue. It was just that old fashioned thing called patriotism and it stumped Mayer. It was a new experience to have an actor come and tell him that he would not be able to appear in any more Metro movies because he was joining the armed forces. He could hardly tell Stewart he was doing the wrong thing. As his wholesome entertainments showed he had always believed strongly in Americanism and patriotism. When he began the sentence: 'Jimmy, we might not even get into this war ... ' his voice trailed off in embarrassment. He averted his eyes as the actor gave him one of his most innocent of glances.

The only case Mayer felt he could put with any conviction was that film stars served their country best by remaining in movies and lifting morale through their performances. Stewart acknowledged the point, but remained unmoved. Even Mayer's last throw, namely the great plans he had for Stewart, fell on stony ground. Not even the chance to star in a remake of *Smilin' Through*, to feature with Spencer Tracy in a version of Louis Bromfield's *Bombay Nights* or to appear in a large-scale film of his own called *Wings On His Back*, made any difference. Stewart's mind was made up. Mayer simply had to give in gracefully. He instructed his publicity chiefs to make as much as they could out of the James Stewart leaving party and wished the actor well. The publicity machine duly went into overdrive, ensuring that every one of the studio's most glamorous female stars was photographed kissing the shyest guy in town.

For Stewart it wasn't having to face Mayer that was his biggest problem. It was his own skinny frame. He had been too thin when he'd arrived in Hollywood some six years before, and now he was too thin for the Army. In November of the previous year he'd been turned down because he was only 140lbs, 10lb too light for his height of 6ft.4in. The only solution was to fatten up which, previous experience had taught him, was no easy matter. To put the extra padding on his bones required by Army regulations he ate spaghetti twice a day and stuffed himself with other fattening foods. Stewart's close friend, MGM executive Bill Grady, recalled:

> Jimmy went down for the physical and I was ready to take him in a studio car. But he refused to let me take him in the limousine. He went by bus instead leaving me with egg on my face. I tailed him to the place where they looked over army candidates. I waited and when a medical officer came out I asked him if Jimmy had made it. The officer told me he'd made it by one ounce. What the officer didn't know was that Jim was so determined to make the weight that he hadn't been to the bathroom for thirty-six hours. It had been torture, but it put him over.'[1]

On 22 March 1941, some eight months before Pearl Harbour, James Stewart was duly inducted as a private into the Army Air Force. The newsreels made the most of the event photographing him as he joined up along with other men from all walks of life, but if they thought they were in for a bonanza of Stewart army publicity they quickly found that that was not to be the case. Stewart requested no interviews and no publicity of any kind. Acting was behind him, at least for the moment. All he wished for now was to get on with the job of being Private 0-433 2I0. He received his first salary cheque after a month. It amounted to $21. He mailed Hayward his ten per cent – $2.10. Hayward immediately had it framed.

Footnote

1. *Saturday Evening Post* (September 1951)

7 Far More Than a Celluloid Soldier

'They used to relate to him as though he
was a movie star for a while, then they'd
realise he was one of the boys.'
                                    Walter Matthau

To the fliers of the 445th Bombing Group it all seemed a bit
unreal at first – to hear the voice of James Stewart coming
over the intercom at 27,000ft. Just a few nights before
many of them had been relaxing in small British cinemas
watching him entertain them in old scratched prints of
Destry, *Mr Smith Goes to Washington* and *The Philadelphia
Story*.

On a bombing raid over Germany, however, it was a
very different matter. The voice was controlled, the
instructions precise and the enunciation was perfect:
'Stewart to crew, Stewart to crew. Low on oxygen. From
now on we're registering on the enemy radar screens. The
Luftwaffe are already warming up for us. So watch your
chatter. Let's not tell 'em anymore than we have to.' It had
taken Stewart nearly three years to reach the point when
he could issue such commands. The early years of the war
had been something of a let down and for a time it seemed
as though he was destined to sit out the war in the States.

At first the Army had wanted him behind a desk. The
offer was met with a polite but firm refusal. That was *not*
why he had joined up, Stewart told them. Training to
become an aircraft mechanic was more to his liking. So too
was flying and testing four-engine bombers. It was the
next assignment that was the hardest to take: instructing
young bomber pilots on the intricacies of flying fortresses.
It was important, vital work and he was good at it. He
understood planes, he knew how they worked and he was

good with men, but rather than train pilots for action in Europe, he would much rather have gone himself.

So casual and relaxing was his lifestyle that he even managed to fit in regular visits to Hollywood. He appeared in uniform to present Gary Cooper with his Oscar for *Sergeant York* in February 1942. Four months later he was on radio with Katharine Hepburn in an adaptation of *The Philadelphia Story*. The Army also made use of his artistic talents, assigning him to narrate two documentaries. The first, *Winning Your Wings* was about the Army Air Corps, the second *Fellow Americans*, dealt with the implications of the raid on Pearl Harbour.

He eventually got into the war when the heavy losses suffered by the bomber groups raiding Germany caused the Army to call for reinforcements. Stewart was one of those who received the call. In November 1943 he arrived in Tibenham, Norfolk, England. England was to become his home for the next three years.

Word quickly got round that Captain James Stewart was 'lucky'. When crews went out with him they returned. There were no heavy casualties. You were safe with Stewart. His B-24 Liberator was called 'Nine Yanks And A Jerk! It led nearly twenty bombing raids over Germany in 1944. On all of them Stewart felt the same strange mix of exhilaration and dread. The exhilaration he had always experienced when high in the sky above the clouds. The dread was something new – the feeling that he might make a mistake that would cost the lives of his men. He had risen from private to captain since joining the Army Air Corps and he knew the planes he was flying like the back of his hand. But there was always the chance, the possibility of that one moment when, through tiredness or worry or some other reason, he might make a slip. He said later:

I did wonder about it lots of times but you had to put it out of your mind as quickly as possible. All of us did. Once you were up in the air you had to. Afterwards, when you had got back to base, you did think about it for a few seconds and you worried. But, before you knew it, you were back up there again.

Real fear came to him suddenly one night, without warning. Morale was low and the High Command was pushing hard. It was one raid after another – a crucial part of the War. Stewart said:

I was really afraid of what the dawn might bring. Our group had suffered several casualties during the day and the next morning at dawn I was going to have to lead my squadron out again, deep into Germany. I got to imagining what might happen and I feared the worst. Fear is an insidious and deadly thing; it can warp judgment, freeze reflexes, breed mistakes. And worse, it's contagious. I could feel my own fear and I knew that if it wasn't checked it could infect my crew members.

Stewart did check it. He went to Chapel.

I guess it was because I kept being reminded that life can be short that I turned to religion. If you think you might die at any moment you think more about the hereafter. Sometimes, during a scary moment in the skies, I would remember the 91st Psalm my father had taught me. I went to Chapel regularly. It was a bad period. Many men I flew with were being killed in action. Religion meant a lot to me for the rest of the war.

Although he was known for his luck and good judgement, Stewart had more than his share of close calls. Once, a mix-up on the intercom caused him to release his bombs and erase the wrong target. On another occasion he was part of the Eighth Air Force attack on the German aircraft industry at Brunswick. It was a massive raid that knocked out many vital targets.

Stewart was leading the second formation that day. On the return home he noticed that the lead group was thirty degrees off course. He called the squadron leader. 'You're wrong,' came the reply. 'We're on course. Stay with us!' Stewart had two options. He could switch to another squadron that he knew was on course. That way his own group would be certain to get back safely. Or he could obey orders and stick with the group he was certain would be prey to enemy fighters. He chose the latter course.

The Luftwaffe struck just twenty-eight miles south of Paris. Sixty Messerschmitts and Folkwulfs dived at the squadron. The lead plane plunged downwards. More B-24s followed. The attack was swift and merciless. Some pilots escaped, baling out deep into France. Others, trapped in their planes burned or died as the planes exploded. Stewart's following group was luckier. It survived the attack and no lives were lost. The group limped home, but it had been a close run thing. For his part in the raid Stewart was later awarded the Distinguished Flying Cross.

One of the jokes that went the rounds in the mission huts of the 445th Bombing Group was that you were safer with Jimmy Stewart at 25,000ft than you were with him on the ground. Stewart had insisted that he receive no Hollywood type publicity during his years in the service and the Army had been careful to respect his wishes. To the men serving with him in England, however, there was no getting away from the fact that his real and screen persona were often one and the same. Certainly the staff of one of the wing stations must have thought they were watching an old Jimmy Stewart movie when he paid them a visit in a Cub airplane used by the wing staff to hop short distances from base to base. Stewart tried to land the tiny plane in a twenty-five-mile-per-hour breeze. It wouldn't adhere to the ground so he decided that the only way he could make certain the plane would stay put was by flipping it over on its back. It worked but his extrication from the inverted position caused much amusement among the willing but mostly untactful pilots who rushed forward to free him.

There was also another problem. Although he could successfully navigate and bring back a bombing group from Germany, the English road system always remained a mystery to him. Once he got lost driving from Tibenham to wing headquarters, a distance of just five miles. On a more ambitious effort from London to Norwich he finally pulled up in Birmingham.

Stewart saw out his war as a colonel and a group operations officer of the 453rd Group in Buckinghamshire. By then his bombing missions were over and he had the difficult and strenuous task of helping to rebuild the group which had suffered heavy losses in personnel and needed bolstering with pilots from the other groups. The lion's share of the rebuilding fell to Stewart. He saw to it that new crews were properly trained and supervised. He excelled at briefings. He knew how to get the attention of every man in the room and hold it. There were no dramatics, but his training as an actor served him well. One who went along to listen to the familiar voice was the young, would-be actor Walter Matthau. He said:

> He was a flier and a lieutenant colonel and I was only a staff sergeant. I used to go to the briefings just to listen to him, just to hear him do his Jimmy Stewart. I watched the way the new crews would relate to him. They used to relate to him as though he were a movie star for a while then they'd forget about all that and realize he was one of the boys. He was marvellous to watch.[1]

When it finally came time to return home in September 1945 Stewart was exhausted both mentally and physically. Like most men who had survived the conflict, he had seen things he would never discuss then or later. The war had left its scars. The sheer horror of watching men die in burning planes, trapped in cockpits or watching clusters of bombs wipe out railyards and sometimes hundreds of people, stayed with him.

His decorations were numerous: the Air Medal, the Distinguished Flying Cross with Oak Leaf Cluster, the Croix de Guerre with Palm and seven battle stars. He had flown more than 1,800 flying hours.

More than any other Hollywood star, James Stewart became the real thing – a genuine American serviceman. Many other figures from the film world served in various branches of the Armed Forces – Gable, Robert Taylor, Tyrone Power, Robert Montgomery. There were many too who saw action. Wayne Morris was a naval aviator who shot down many Japanese; William Wyler lost the hearing in one ear when he went on a bombing mission to film his documentary *Memphis Belle*; John Huston braved enemy fire with the common soldier when filming *The Battle of San*

Pietro; Sterling Hayden fought with the partisans in Yugoslavia. It was Stewart, however, who at the war's end emerged as the one star who had submerged himself completely and cut himself off from the luxurious world he had known before the war. And that made the return that much more difficult.

When the war eventually came to an end in August 1945 Stewart found himself heading for home and wondering whether the break had been too long for him ever to return to the movies. It had been five years since he had made a film. He was a very mature thirty-seven. Specks of white flecked his hair. The business he had enjoyed so much in the late thirties now seemed trivial and unimportant. As he left the shores of Britain several questions kept nagging away at him. Did he really want to return to movies? Would he be accepted? Was acting really a serious enough profession considering what he had seen in the war? Above all, would he be able to settle and readjust?

He was still unsure of the answers when he arrived back in New York in September, 1945.

Footnote

1. *American Film Institute Life Achievement Award* (February 1980)

8   It's a Wonderful Life

'From that moment Jimmy decided that if
he was going to be an actor then he was
going to be the best there was.'

Frank Capra

Louis B. Mayer was usually unlucky in his dealings with James Stewart and on a late September morning in 1945 he was faring no better than usual. The last time the actor had stood in his office had been when he'd asked for a release to join the army. Now, with the war over, he wanted out for good.

Mayer glowered at the gangling and distinctly nervous Stewart who was only too well aware of how quickly the MGM boss could be roused to anger. He recalled and then tried to forget an occasion when Mayer had become so bored with an editor's dreary account of a new novel that he'd eventually seized the story editor by the throat and tried to choke him.

Mayer drummed his fingers on the desk. 'That son-of-a-bitch agent of yours put you up to this didn't he?' he snapped. 'That bastard Hayward.' Stewart did his perfect impression of Jimmy Stewart, widening his eyes and slowly formulating a kind of helpless shrug. He said nothing. 'Don't interrupt. The bastard's been trying to get even ever since I had him barred from the lot. You heard about that I suppose.' He glanced at Stewart's face for a reaction. Stewart remained impassive. In many ways the ordeal was more harrowing than flying B-24s over Germany. Mayer said bluntly: 'I could insist that you stay. You know that don't you. You still owe me two years on your contract.'

'With respect Mr Mayer, I don't think I do.'

The award-winning *You Can't Take It With You* (1938) with
Stewart as the son of business tycoon Edward Arnold (left) and
Lionel Barrymore (right) as his future father-in-law

Stewart as the idealistic young Jefferson Smith with the corrupt
senator, Claude Rains in *Mr Smith Goes to Washington* (1939)

Romance with Katharine Hepburn in *The Philadelphia Story* (1940). The film earned Stewart the Academy Award as best actor of the year

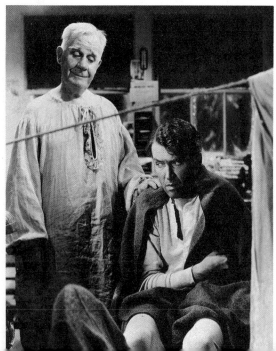

It's a Wonderful Life (1946), although Stewart clearly doesn't think so in this scene with guardian angel, Henry Travers

A change of pace and a change of style as the professor of Nietzschean philosophy grappling with pupil Farley Granger in *Rope* (1948)

The famed single set of *Rope* (1948) scene of Hitchcock's ten-minute take. The set was created at the Warner Bros. studio in Hollywood

As the peace-loving frontiersman Tom Jefstanders in
Broken Arrow (1950)

The new-look Stewart, vengeful and violent in *Winchester 73*
(1950) – the film that turned Stewart into a major star in
the fifties

'Now Elwood there isn't really an invisible rabbit is there?'
Josephine Hull desperately tries to ignore the obvious in
Harvey (1950)

Stewart with film star passenger Marlene Dietrich
and stewardess Glynis Johns in *No Highway* (1951)

James Stewart and June Allyson – one of the most popular romantic teams of the post-war years – in *The Glenn Miller Story* (1953)

One of the highlights of *The Glenn Miller Story* (1953). Stewart with Trummy Young, Louis Armstrong, Cozy Cole, Gene Krupa, Barney Bigard, Arvel Shaw and Marty Napoleon

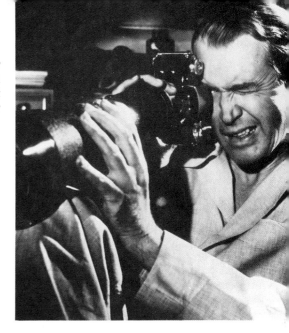

Stewart in *Rear Window* (1954) confined to a wheelchair but suspecting murder

With perhaps the most glamorous of all his leading ladies, Grace Kelly in the Hitchcock thriller *Rear Window* (1954)

Out West again for Anthony Mann in *The Man from Laramie*
(1955)

Mayer's face grew red: 'This is your home for God's sake. You started here. You won your goddam Oscar at this studio. Don't you have any *loyalty?*' His fingers clenched into a threatening fist and this time he banged heavily on his desk. 'It's that lousy de Havilland woman. Ever since she took Jack Warner to court all of you damned actors think you can get out of your contracts. Well, you know what that would do? It would ruin the business. Not only for us but also for people like you. Ever think about that. You oughta try it sometime.'

Stewart waited. He knew Mayer had nowhere to go and was just blustering. De Havilland was indeed behind it all. Just four months earlier she had won a court case against Warner establishing that a seven-year contract was just that. If an actor or an actress went on suspension for refusing certain roles that time could not be added to a star's contract as it had been in the past. No longer could a seven-year contract extend to eight, nine, even ten years. Stewart reasoned that his years in the Air Force should be taken into account, that he had now completed his seven-year contract with Metro and that he owed them nothing.

Mayer snapped at him fiercely: 'What are you going to do if you leave here? This is still the best studio in town. It's tough out there nowadays, much tougher than it used to be. You actors need the safety of the studios. You'll find that out.'

It was the first thing Mayer had said that made Stewart think twice. He hesitated but then put his case once again: 'It's nothing against Metro Mr Mayer. It's just that I'm not even sure I want to carry on acting anymore. I need time. And if I do carry on in the business then I'd prefer to go freelance. A lot of other guys are doing it.'

'They won't last,' growled Mayer. He shook his head. He had better things to do with his time than argue all day with rebellious actors. Such as making MGM an even better studio than it had been before the war. If Stewart wanted no part of it then so be it. Minutes later Stewart drove from Culver City a free man.

Mayer had been right when he'd said that Leland Hayward had put him up to it. The agent's first advice to

Stewart when he arrived back in Hollywood was that he should leave MGM. He explained the importance of the de Havilland case and suggested that Stewart would do better if he struck out on his own.

There was a little more to it than that, however. Hayward had his own reasons for wanting to put one over on Mayer. A few months earlier he had signed the handsome young newcomer Gregory Peck as one of his clients. After Peck's performance in Metro's *Valley of Decision* Mayer had tried to sign the actor to a seven-year contract. Hayward advised Peck otherwise. He went into overdrive, wheeling and dealing his way across Hollywood and securing one of the most lucrative deals in Hollywood history – Peck's services to be shared among four studios for staggering sums.

Mayer was furious. He believed he had the God-given right to sign any star he chose. He banned Hayward from the lot. Stewart's case was tailor-made for revenge. It would allow the actor to make better deals and also make Mayer squirm. Hayward, who loved nothing more than tormenting the moguls, had the last word. When Stewart walked out of Metro he knew he had won. Afterwards Mayer spoke of Hayward only in terms of revilement.

For Stewart, freelancing brought with it all manner of uncertainties. For the first time since he had arrived in Hollywood he was on his own and questioning whether the boyish, awkward charm that had stood him in such good stead before the war would still hold good five years later.

His chance to find out came late in 1945 when he received a telephone call from Frank Capra asking if he would be interested in discussing a film the director was preparing for his new company Liberty Films. Like Stewart, Capra had been away from mainstream cinema for several years, serving in the US Army as a colonel and making the celebrated *Why We Fight* series of war documentaries. His partners in the Liberty Films enterprise were fellow directors George Stevens and William Wyler and also Sam Briskin. The deal was that the three directors would each make three films of their own choice all of which would be distributed by the RKO

Studio. RKO would pay them a salary in exchange for the film-makers putting up their own funds. RKO would also provide the studio facilities. It was really a kind of post-war United Artists with Sam Briskin acting as vice president and treasurer.

Capra was the first of the three to go into production. Nervous and unsure of himself he would have preferred to have eased his way back into film-making with a couple of quickie westerns, but he knew that his reputation and the three Oscars on his sideboard hardly allowed for that. After discarding two or three possible projects he settled for a little fairy-tale called 'The Greatest Gift'.

It reminded him in many ways of the social comedies he had made so successfully at Columbia before the war. Its hero was George Bailey – an ordinary small-town man who is anxious to see the world and make a name for himself as an architect. Events conspire to keep him at home in Bedford Falls where he marries, has a family and is forced to watch as the years and opportunities pass him by. When, eventually, he loses faith and contemplates suicide he is saved by a guardian angel who reveals to him how different the town would have been had he not been born and not spent his life helping others.

Capra kept asking himself whether the story was really as silly and schmaltzy as it sounded and found himself saying 'yes' to both questions. He also kept reminding himself that it would not be an easy story to bring to the screen and that three Hollywood screenwriters, among them Dalton Trumbo and Clifford Odets, had been defeated by it when RKO had originally purchased the story for Cary Grant. Yet there was something about 'The Greatest Gift' that fascinated him. He bought the rights for just $50,000 and decided to test things out on Stewart.

It was a curious scene that was played out in Sam Briskin's apartment in late November, 1945. Capra hadn't told the story of a film to an actor for four years and Stewart hadn't heard one from a director for six. Both men were tense, both nervous and unsure of themselves.

To Capra, Stewart seemed remote, even bored. In Stewart's eyes, Capra was a little over the top and confused in his telling, but he sat and listened patiently.

Capra ploughed on with the story realizing that with every sentence the whole thing sounded sillier and sillier. When he got to the point when he had to say 'when the angel, who's called Clarence, saves George's life he gets his wings' he stopped suddenly and collapsed on the sofa. The story seemed to evaporate into thin air. 'Goddam-it Jimmy, I haven't got a story. This is the lousiest piece of cheese I ever heard. Forget it Jimmy, forget it.' With that the meeting ended.

Two weeks later Stewart called Capra on the telephone: 'Frank, this is Jimmy. I just thought I'd tell you that if you want me to do a movie in which I try to commit suicide and am saved by an angel called Clarence who hasn't won his wings, I'm your boy. Anything Frank. Anything.'

Stewart's confidence in the project did the trick. Some four months later, on 8 April 1946, star and director embarked on the film, now retitled *It's a Wonderful Life*, that was to become one of the enduring classics of American cinema. When the Hollywood press began enquiring about the content of his comeback film, Capra, remembering the débâcle in Briskin's apartment, was deliberately vague: 'Oh, well, let's see how it turns out. It's a kinda crazy story with angels and things.'

Stewart also steered clear of discussion. 'I don't pick a story, I pick a director,' he said firmly.

The making of the film put an immense strain on both men. Stewart found himself in front of the cameras for almost seventy consecutive days. It was by far the most demanding role of his career and required him to be even more thorough than usual in his preparation. For much of the time it was a struggle. Even with Capra at the helm he found there was no easy return to movie acting. Mostly he prepared at home and always by himself. He never used a tape recorder. He said later:

I guess there's all different ways of acting and of preparing oneself for the next day's work. I know some actors like to sit around and discuss the scene with the director. Frank Capra didn't seem to care for this. I used to do my own presentation and then, if it didn't work and the director wanted changes, I'd start messing around with it.

Stewart was the only major star in *It's a Wonderful Life*, but Capra made sure that he surrounded him with the strongest supporting cast possible. The lovely young Donna Reed, then at the beginning of her career, played Stewart's adoring wife, Thomas Mitchell featured as the lovable Uncle Billy, Henry Travers was Clarence and Lionel Barrymore the villain of the piece, the crusty old town banker Henry Potter. It was Barrymore who eventually persuaded Stewart that he should forget any thoughts he had about giving up acting and carry on his career as a movie star. Remembered Capra:

> During the filming of *It's a Wonderful Life* Jimmy would sometimes get bouts of depression and tell me that acting seemed silly and unimportant compared to what he had seen in the war. On one occasion he said he thought he would make just the one post-war movie and then quit and perhaps try something in aviation.
>
> Well, Lionel Barrymore felt that acting was one of the greatest professions ever invented and was very out-spoken about it too. One day, he said to me: 'That Jimmy Stewart is good.' 'Yeah,' I said, 'but he's thinking of quitting' and I told him why.
>
> A few days later Barrymore talked to Jimmy and gave him a pitch on acting that would have convinced just about anyone: 'Don't you realize,' he said, 'that you're moving millions of people, shaping their lives, giving them a sense of exaltation. What other profession has that power or can be so important? A bad actor is a bad actor. But acting is among the oldest and noblest professions in the world young man' Stewart took due note of the advice. He never actually said it in so many words, but I think it was from that moment that Jimmy decided that if he was going to be an actor, then he was going to be the best there was.[1]

Capra set himself a punishing schedule for filming *It's a Wonderful Life*. He worked nonstop for six days a week until shooting finished on 27 July 1946. As the weeks ticked by, his enthusiasm for the project grew – and so too did the budget which had originally been set at $1,700,000, but, because of Capra's perfectionism and the prepon-derance of night shots, finished up at $2,800,000. Much,

much too expensive for the first picture of a newly formed independent company.

Nonetheless, as he busied himself in the cutting rooms preparing his film for its pre-Christmas December release, Capra sensed, as he viewed the various rough cuts, that he had pulled it off. The quaint little story had worked after all. *It's a Wonderful Life* seemed every bit as good as his pre-war successes. Perhaps even better. All that would be needed would be some good notices and a healthy first week at the box-office in New York. The rest would follow. Liberty Films would have been launched in style.

Unfortunately things didn't quite work out that way. Stewart received some of the best notices of his career, *The New York Times* critic making a point of noting that he had grown in spiritual stature as well as talent since he had been in the war. The reviews for the film itself, however, were uneven. Some were excellent. James Agee, writing in *The Nation*, called the picture 'One of the most efficient sentimental pieces since *A Christmas Carol*.' But for every favourable notice there were two bad ones. *The New Yorker* savaged the film: 'It's so mincing as to border on baby talk … Henry Travers, God help him, has the job of portraying Mr Stewart's guardian angel. It must have taken a lot out of him.' Bosley Crowther in *The New York Times* admitted the undoubted qualities of the film, but took issue with Capra's idealistic view of life in small-town America: 'The weakness of the picture … is its illusory concept of life. Mr Capra's nice people are charming, his small town is a quite beguiling place and his pattern for solving problems is most optimistic and facile. But somehow they all resemble theatrical attitudes, rather than average realities.'

The split in the reviews was reflected in the film's performance at the box-office. Despite its obvious Christmas appeal it opened 'soft' in New York. At first this was put down to the bitterly cold weather that swept down the Hudson in the middle of December, but it soon became apparent that it was very much the same story right across the country. The picture performed respectably, but no more. After the holidays the drop-off was plain for all to see. By February *The Jolson Story, Till The Clouds Roll By, Lady In The Lake, The Yearling* and *The Best*

Years of Our Lives were all achieving better financial returns.

A bitterly disappointed Capra, accompanied by Stewart, made a whirlwind tour to tub-thump the film. It did little good. The public turned up to see them, but not the picture. Takings continued to fall away. The last hope were the Oscars. Success at the Academy Awards might give the film the financial boost it needed. If not it became apparent to everyone that the film would not get into profit.

The 1947 ceremonies took place at the Shrine Auditorium in Los Angeles on 13 March. Things started badly and got progressively worse. A silent compilation of earlier Oscar-winning films was projected upside down and backwards onto the ceiling instead of the screen. Ronald Reagan, then President of the Screen Actor's Guild and oblivious of the snarl up in the projection room, carried on with the commentary which began: 'This picture embodies the glories of our past, the memories of our present and the inspiration of our future.'

Something else that should have warned the *It's a Wonderful Life* hopefuls that it was not going to be their night was that the bookmakers installed Stewart as hot favourite at 6-5. When he had been favourite for *Mr Smith* just before the war he had lost to Robert Donat. In March 1947 history repeated itself. Fredric March took the acting award for his returning war veteran in William Wyler's *The Best Years of Our Lives*. Wyler's film also picked up another six awards making it easily the top film of the night. *It's a Wonderful Life* which had been nominated in six categories, finished up with nothing. It was a body blow to Capra, Stewart and everyone connected with the film. *It's a Wonderful Life* lost half a million dollars.

Capra later went on record as saying that the main reason he had been so attracted to *It's a Wonderful Life* was because its theme stated over and over again that no man is a failure. In 1946/7 it seemed that post-war audiences couldn't have cared less. Capra-esque philosophies were of little interest. Six years of war had rendered Capra and his cheerful Americana redundant. Said Capra: 'Perhaps I had too much faith in the human race in the pictures that I made. Maybe they did show things as they should have been rather than as they were. People called me a kind of movie *Pollyanna* and I guess maybe I was.' Stewart has always felt a little non-plussed by the film's failure:

> The only thing I've been able to come up with is that people had just been through a war and that this was not quite what they were looking for. The picture, even though there was a comedy side to it and everything, was really a very serious picture. There was a dark side to it. I think movie audiences wanted Red Skelton, slapstick comedy, westerns, escapism. We were finished with the war. Maybe it was just the wrong time to make the picture.'

It's a Wonderful Life more or less finished Capra and proved to be the death knoll for Liberty Films which folded just two years later. Yet, ironically, it is now regarded as one of the most complete of American films – a monument to American film-making at its best. It is quintessential Americana, a unique study of small-town life, brimming over with Capra's vigour and optimism. It does have a rosy-eyed view of the human condition, of that there is no doubt, but audiences, young and old, still respond to it as a beautiful evocation of old-time American values, hoping perhaps that even in contemporary America those values may not have entirely vanished. Time and distance may have lent enchantment, but *It's a Wonderful Life* remains a quite unique achievement.

Had audiences taken to it when it really mattered Capra might well have survived as a major film-maker. As it was, he made just half a dozen mediocre films in the ensuing twenty years then retired.

For Stewart, the outlook in mid 1947 was similarly bleak. There had been moments in *It's a Wonderful Life* when he had revealed hidden depths as a performer. His perfectly controlled underplaying as he reflects his frustration at being kept in his 'crummy little town', his quite magical love scene with Donna Reed as he tries to resist her charms while occupied on the telephone, and his almost total breakdown in the bar at the end of the film displayed an actor of considerable range and subtlety.

The fact remained, however, that *It's a Wonderful Life* had been a commercial flop. He had needed a commercial hit. He had little idea of what to do next. He imagined he could hear Louis B. Mayer laughing to himself in his large office over at Metro. He couldn't really blame him – He would have done the same.

Footnote

1. *Esquire*, Peter Bogdanovich (July 1966)

9 Hathaway, Hitchcock and The Ten-minute Take

'I simply wasn't getting across anymore. I knew I had to toughen up.'

James Stewart

Stewart had heard many unnerving tales about Henry Hathaway. Gary Cooper and Hank Fonda had both worked for the director in the pre-war days at Paramount and warned that he could be salty, bad-tempered and very tough. 'The meanest man in Hollywood,' said Hank Fonda. 'At least that's what the technicians call him.'

Stewart's chance to discover whether all this was true occurred in the Fall of 1947 when he began filming *Call Northside 777*. It wasn't long before he realized that the rumours were by no means exaggerated. Cameramen, technicians, property men and others were all victims of Hathaway's tongue-lashing. So too were the supporting actors and bit players. Only the stars escaped being balled out.

During the shooting of *Call Northside 777* it was a luckless bit player who caught the full force of Hathaway's fury. He had messed up a simple scene in which he had to look at a photograph and then deny, silently, that he recognized the man in the picture. It wasn't difficult, but he couldn't get it right.

Hathaway controlled his temper by chewing furiously on his cigar. 'Just look at the photograph, *then* shake your head,' he growled with growing impatience.

The bit player seemed to have a problem.

'Why do I have to shake my head?'

'What the hell does it matter? Read the script. Haven't you *read* the script. Just do the fuckin' scene. DO IT!'

Members of the crew shuffled about and suddenly found interesting things to do with their fingernails. The bit player did his best to remain calm.

'If you didn't shout Mr Hathaway I could concentrate better, perhaps if ...'

'I'M NOT SHOUTING!'

The actor pulled himself together.

'Son-of-a-bitch,' muttered Hathaway. 'I wanna get this picture *finished* for Chrissake. ACTION.'

The bit player looked at the photograph and dutifully shook his head.

'CUT! PRINT!'

The technicians breathed again and began setting up the next scene. Hathaway chewed on his cigar and ordered a cup of tea.

The vibrancy of a Hathaway set was just the tonic Stewart needed after the commercial failure of *It's a Wonderful Life*. Things were very different with Hathaway than they had been with Capra. The director was quick to anger, but there was an honest, no-nonsense approach to his work that Stewart admired.

He also enjoyed Hathaway's company off set. He found him a robust, personable companion with a sense of humour and a refreshing matter-of-fact attitude to life. Stewart certainly needed someone to listen to his problems and to keep his enthusiasm on the boil. Not only had he suffered a disappointment with *It's a Wonderful Life*, but he'd compounded his mistake by following it up with *Magic Town*, a whimsical sub-Capra piece about a down-on-his-luck pollster who exploits the opinions of the inhabitants of the one perfectly average town in all America.

The premise was intriguing and the film would have worked well as a satire especially if a film-maker like Preston Sturges had been at the helm. Instead, Bill Wellman was assigned as director. He was good at most things, especially westerns, action and aviation movies. The one thing he was not good at was films about small-town America. The movie was a dud. After its release Wellman was the first to agree: 'It stunk. If you think *Magic Town* has anything good about it, there's something wrong with you.'

Stewart's confidence took yet another knock shortly afterwards when he was interviewed by a journalist who had been commissioned to write a career article for *The New York Times*. The journalist wasted no time on niceties. He laid it straight on the line: 'Mr Stewart, I have to tell you right off that this thing is going to be called "The Rise and Fall of James Stewart".' Before the startled actor could interject the journalist had fired off the first question: Did he, Stewart, think he would be able to survive in post-war Hollywood?

The interview was a sobering experience and forced Stewart into a drastic rethink. He said later:

> I knew, right then and there, that I was going to have to do something. I just couldn't go on hemming and hawing which I realized I'd overdone at times. I looked at some of my old pictures and couldn't believe what I was watching. One of them, *Born To Dance*, made me want to vomit. I simply wasn't getting across anymore. I knew I had to toughen up.[1]

Which is why, in 1947, he found himself working for Henry Hathaway on *Call Northside 777*. It was an interesting and provocative picture, another in the series of semi-documentary thrillers produced by the Fox studio since the war. All were distinguished by the fact that they were based on true stories and photographed, as far as possible, on the actual locations where the events occurred. Hathaway, who liked nothing more than getting out of the studio to take charge of the second-unit work, had directed most of them.

Call Northside 777 differed from the others in that it was a newspaper story. Photographed in the streets, back alleys and sleazy bars of Chicago, it cast Stewart as a reporter who patiently and methodically goes about securing a pardon for a man who, in 1932, had been accused of murdering a cop and then wrongfully imprisoned for thirteen years. Lee J. Cobb co-starred as his liberal-minded editor and Richard Conte as the convicted man.

Stewart had played journalists before – cynical ones, romantic ones, absent-minded ones – but never a real-life reporter so at least the picture allowed him to break some new ground. With the reporter – James P. McGuire (renamed McNeal in the movie) – constantly on set as consultant and technical adviser he was able to play down his mannerisms and dig deeper than usual into his characterization.

Working with Hathaway also helped. Stewart escaped Hathaway's cursing and bullying because he was the kind of actor Hathaway admired. Like Cooper and Fonda and Wayne he belonged to the natural 'born-for-what-they-are' school of performer. There was no bullshit about him. Hathaway knew he was reliable and that he would deliver.

The performers the director really detested were the young method-style actors who demanded motivation for every scene. Hathaway would have no truck with any of it. 'Don't ask questions: It's a load of crap,' he would yell at any performer who dared to query a role in detail. 'Fuck the motivation, just do the fuckin' scene,' he told a young Dennis Hopper, reputedly more than seventy times during the filming of a scene in the western *From Hell To Texas*. Hopper walked off the set three times, but three times he was forced to return, to argue yet again. Robert Duvall was another who found the going tough when he worked with Hathaway on John Wayne's Oscar-winning western *True Grit*.

Yet for all the bullying and the bristling obscenities the one thing that always stood Hathaway in good stead was that he was fast. Because of the fear he created on set his pictures came in on time. He never bothered with rushes because he knew exactly what he had shot and what it would look like. Unlike Capra who believed the director was king and should have his name above the title, Hathaway believed a movie was a job of work. A veteran of the silent days, he was a studio man through and through. When he had completed one film he would take a short break and then go on to the next. It was his proud boast that he never once turned down an assignment during his entire career in Hollywood.

Call Northside 777 was one of his best. It was also a good film for Stewart. The notices were enthusiastic. Some were outstanding. Bosley Crowther wrote in *The New York Times*: 'Call Northside 777 is a slick piece of melodrama that combines a suspenseful mystery story with a vivid realistic pictorial style and which is winningly acted by James Stewart as the reporter sleuth.'

C.A. Lejeune in *The Observer* in London, also attested to the film's values, but reserved most of her praise for Stewart: 'Mr Stewart has really got under the skin of a journalist who starts an enquiry indifferently as just one more story in a round of assignments, then finds the business taking hold of him until he is utterly possessed by it. It is a fine performance, all the better because it has no obvious tricks of showmanship, and he gets splendid help from Henry Hathaway's direction.'

Another picture with Hathaway at this stage of his career would have done Stewart no harm at all, but it was at this point that the disadvantages as well as the advantages of being a freelance came to the fore. Hathaway was duly signed by Fox to make his next studio picture, a whaling picture called *Down to the Sea in Ships*, whilst Stewart was forced to keep his hand in with a pair of comedies that no self-respecting star, especially one of his standing, should even remotely have considered.

One was *You Gotta Stay Happy*, a poor man's *It Happened One Night* with millionairess Joan Fontaine on the run from her husband and finding solace with ex-army pilot Stewart. The other was *On Our Merry Way*, an indifferent portmanteau movie made up of several unrelated episodes, one of which featured Stewart and Hank Fonda as a couple of jazz musicians trying to fix an amateur dance contest. Neither film did any business. All the advantages gained by the toughened up Stewart of *Northside* were immediately lost.

Stewart also began to realize that it wasn't just the problems of his own screen personality that he had to worry about, it was also the rapidly growing stature of several of the newer American stars who had emerged since the war. Gregory Peck was one. He offered the greatest threat in that he provided audiences with the same kind of All-American virtue and honesty that Stewart himself had supplied in the late thirties. There were others too who were also making their mark: Kirk Douglas for instance, all ferocity and dimpled chin, the laconic sleepy-eyed Robert Mitchum and the athletic Burt Lancaster. All, in their own way offered serious competition, not only through their acting talents but also because of their age. All were in their early thirties. Stewart was rapidly approaching forty.

Luckily Stewart's confidence was rekindled at just the right moment by an out-of-the-blue offer from a director he much admired – Alfred Hitchcock.

Together with Britain's Sidney Bernstein, Hitchcock had just formed an independent company called Transatlantic Pictures. He had chosen as his first production a version of Patrick Hamilton's 1929 stage play *Rope*. It was a macabre little piece about two students who are influenced by the Nietzschean theories taught to them by their philosophy teacher. They murder a fellow student just for the thrill of it, and then have guests over for a cocktail party, serving food from the top of a trunk in which the body is concealed.

For the part of the professor, Hitchcock had tried first for Cary Grant with whom he had worked twice before. Grant, however, was unable to get a release from his RKO contract so Hitch went after Stewart instead. The actor, although flattered, was doubtful about the role. A break from his homespun image was one thing; a totally un-Stewart like part was something else. Would audiences really accept him as a professor whose theories incite students to murder? Hitchcock was confident that they would. He had cast against type before he told Stewart. It always worked.

Stewart still wasn't entirely convinced but, after some additional persuasion from his new agent Lew Wasserman – Hayward having departed for a theatrical career as a Broadway producer – he eventually agreed to the project, driving a hard bargain, asking and getting $300,000 for his services.

The aspect of the film that fascinated Stewart the most was that Hitchcock was going to shoot the picture in 'long takes' which meant that he would abandon all editing techniques and photograph the film in takes of ten minutes, the maximum amount of film (1000ft) held in the camera. As the picture took place on the one set – the students' Manhattan penthouse apartment during a single evening – Hitchcock planned to shoot the film in just eight takes. In other words, eighty minutes of screen time. It was to say the least, a bizarre idea. Despite the originality of the approach there was no way that Hitchcock could liven things up if the film got bogged down in too much talk as it frequently did. All he could hope for were quality performances to hold the interest, and these he didn't get. Stewart was ill-at-ease in the central role and Farley Granger and John Dall made little impression as the unbalanced young killers.

The result was a numbingly boring film that pleased no one. For all the cinematic excitement that was on offer audiences might just as well have been in a theatre watching a stage play. The most interesting thing about *Rope* was the filming itself. Indeed, during shooting Stewart jokily told Hitchcock: 'I think you missed the boat on this one Hitch. You should have surrounded the whole set with bleachers and sold tickets so that people could watch this amazing routine with the walls moving and all the technical tricks. Because all of that is much more interesting than what we're saying.'

Stewart was right. The complexities of the filming were fascinating and also proved to be quite a strain on the actors. Any fluffing around the seven or eight minute mark meant that all the film in the camera was wasted and the scene would have to be begun again. Things went wrong on the very first day when Hitch reached eight of his ten minutes only to find the camera taking in a couple of technicians by mistake. Luckily it was an isolated incident. Mistakes were rare. They had to be, they were too costly.

Stewart found the filming of *Rope* to be both a fascinating and a daunting experience. Later, when recalling the shooting of the film, he said:

I think all of us in the cast were intrigued by the technique although there were a few who expressed quite a lot of doubts about it.

Hitch was totally absorbed in it all. He had the walls mounted on rubber wheels so they wouldn't make a noise. But that didn't work because they *were* noisy and so was the camera moving around all the time.

After the first day or so he found it impossible to use the sound. So, instead of shooting it all and then have us loop the dialogue afterwards, he did something I've never seen done before. He did one take for the camera but with no microphones. Then he took all the cameras away and replaced them with ten moving microphones on booms. Then we'd do the same scene following exactly the same moves, for sound only.

During the filming the camera was on tracks. Everything about the filming – the lighting, the scenery and the camera moves were crucial. They even had to have an extra man on the camera crew. They used to call him 'The Pointer' because he held something like a long fishing rod and would point to the next numbered move for the camera and where it should be.

Unfortunately, all this technical virtuosity brought little but stifled yawns from those audiences who did venture out to see the movie. The critics were lukewarm both about the film and Stewart's performance. 'Miscast' was the majority verdict which didn't surprise Stewart in the least. The box office ticked over, just, but for most movie-goers the entertainment on offer was distinctly meagre.

Hitchcock later admitted that the use of the 'ten-minute' take had been an error of judgment on his part. In an interview with Francois Truffaut he said:

> I undertook *Rope* as a stunt. That's the only way I can describe it. I don't know how I came to indulge in it. When I look back I realize that it was quite nonsensical because I was breaking with my own theories on the importance of cutting and montage for the visual narration of a story ... As an experiment *Rope* may be forgiven but it was definitely a mistake.[2]

Rope was shot quickly on a single sound stage at Warner Brothers over a period of just eighteen days. There were ten days of rehearsals. The film cost 1½ million dollars and eventually made a small profit, but it did little to enhance the reputations of either its director or star. Like Stewart, Hitch had struck a fallow period after enjoying a string of successes earlier in the decade. He wouldn't regain his form until the 50s when he would team again with Stewart, this time on a series of movie thrillers that were destined to become classics. In 1948 though, it's doubtful whether either man would have given much in the way of odds about them ever working together again. *Rope* had been an interesting experience, but hardly a rewarding one.

In the meantime, as Stewart totted up the sum of his screen achievements since the war, the prospects were anything but encouraging. The items in red ink far outnumbered those in black. *It's a Wonderful Life, Magic Town, You Gotta Stay Happy* and *On Our Merry Way* had all been financial flops. *Rope* had managed to break even. Only *Call Northside 777* had been a success. Whichever way one looked at it the balance was wrong. An end of term report might have read: Tries hard but still out of touch. Future prospects: Uncertain. Marks out of ten: six. Needs a hit badly.

Footnotes

1. *Esquire*, Peter Bogdanovich (July 1966)
2. *Hitchcock*, Francois Truffaut, Simon and Schuster (1968)

10   Marriage and Gloria

'I knew he was Hollywood's most eligible
bachelor but nothing had been said about
him being so shy. He hardly said
anything all evening.

Gloria Stewart

'Bogart Weds Bacall' ... *'Robert Mitchum Arrested On
Marijuana Charge'* ... *Rita Hayworth Leaves Columbia For
Prince Aly Khan'* ... *'Ingrid Bergman Bears The Illegitimate
Child Of Roberto Rossellini'*

Compared with these post-war 'media events', the
continuing bachelor status of James Stewart was of only
minor concern to the Hollywood press. They'd already got
plenty of mileage out of the subject in the thirties. They
had even tried to rekindle interest when Stewart had
returned from the army in 1945. 'He's Back Girls –
Hollywood's Most Eligible Bachelor is up for Grabs and on
the Loose in Tinseltown' was typical of the magazine
headlines of the time. Once it became obvious, however,
that Stewart was no longer dating leading Hollywood
stars and preferred to keep a low profile, interest in his
marital prospects quickly faded.

June Allyson, who was to be his screen wife in a trio of
successful movies remembered that the Jimmy Stewart of
the late forties was very different to the pre-war Stewart.
She said: 'Jimmy hated being photographed when he was
out with a girl and he seldom took his dates to nightclubs.
Instead, he fed them steak that he had grilled in his own
backyard. If they didn't like that and wanted the limelight
they were not for him.'

The general consensus in Hollywood was that, as he

reached the age of forty, James Maitland Stewart was a confirmed bachelor and quite happy to remain so. Rumours persisted from those who professed to be 'in the know' that the reason he never got married was because he had always been secretly in love with Margaret Sullavan and had never found anyone who might take her place. They remained only rumours, however, and Stewart himself never commented.

One who was always trying to get him married off was Leland Hayward. He never gave up on him and was constantly acting as marriage-broker. When Stewart arrived back after the war and confessed that he was uncertain about continuing as an actor it was Hayward who suggested the best alternative: marriage to a rich girl and then a life of ease. And guess what? He knew exactly the right girl. When Stewart gave him an amused quizzical look Hayward insisted he wasn't joking. 'She's great,' he said. 'One in a million. You'll love her. Take her to dinner and the theatre then marry her. Here's her number. Call her as soon as you can!'

Hayward kept pursuing the matter so vigorously that Stewart felt sure he must be getting his 10% agent's fee if the marriage came off. Partly to keep his friend from badgering him and partly because he had become interested in discovering just who this superwoman might be, Stewart relented. Following Hayward's instructions, he arranged a dinner and a show. The evening was a total disaster. Said Stewart:

> I called her then went and picked her up. I asked a doorman to get a taxi – this was New York – and she said 'Don't you have a car?' That was my first mistake. Then we had dinner and we just didn't seem to have much to talk about. Then, to make matters worse, she ordered something she didn't like. Then we went to the theatre and it wasn't a very good play. After the theatre we had a terrible time getting a cab and in the end she said: 'I think I'd like to go home now.' She said goodbye and left me in the lobby and that was it.

Hayward was bitterly disappointed. He felt his judgement was in question. He couldn't understand it, he said. He was sure they were made for each other. In the end he blamed Stewart for being too shy and not trying hard enough and for not sending any flowers. 'You can't fool around with a thing like this,' he said. 'If you want to get something going you gotta send flowers. Leave it to me. *I'll* send them.'

Hayward duly sent the flowers. It didn't work. Stewart got the bill for what seemed like a thousand roses and never saw superwoman again.

Another of Stewart's longtime friends, MGM casting director Bill Grady, also learned the inside story of one of Stewart's less successful romantic encounters. He remembered:

> There was this pretty, red-headed starlet. He'd been dating her for some time so I asked how the romance was working out. He looked puzzled. That was nothing new. Jimmy often did but this time he looked more so than usual. 'I'm not sure,' he said, 'I just don't seem to understand her.
>
> Later, I found out that they had been parked outside of her house on a moonlit night. The dame felt romantic and said: 'It's so lovely, the trolls must be out tonight!' Now if she'd said elves or pixies or leprechauns Jimmy might have gotten it but trolls didn't register with him at all so he asked: 'Who are The Trolls, your neighbours?' The girl stared at him in amazement, ran inside and slammed the door.[1]

It was Gary Cooper who finally got things moving. Coop was a longtime friend and was well aware of Stewart's taste in women. They would often discuss things when they went fishing or hunting together. Their friendship stemmed from the fact that they had similar personalities, shared the same cracker-barrel philosophies and were masters in the art of slow-talking. Often, even when discussing women, they would simply use 'yep' or 'nope' when holding a conversation. On one occasion they even managed to communicate without using any words at all. Stewart was standing in his front porch when Cooper drove up, pulled over to the side of the road and opened his car door. Stewart waved. Cooper made shooting gestures with his hands. Stewart nodded. Cooper shut the car door and drove off. The invitation to go shooting had been made and accepted.

It was his acceptance of a very different kind of invitation – to an elaborate dinner party at Cooper's house one evening in the summer of 1948 that ultimately changed the course of Stewart's life. Many of Stewart's closest friends were at the party including Henry Hathaway. Stewart was the spare man and Gloria Hatrick McLean, an attractive 31-year-old divorcee and mother of two, the spare woman. An ex-model with brown hair and attractive green eyes, she was not an actress and had no aspirations of becoming one. Her first husband had been the millionaire Edward McLean, jun. to whom she had borne two sons and whose mother Evelyn Walsh McLean owned the famous Hope Diamond. She knew her way round the movie world because her father was the head of the legal staff at MGM.

Gloria had caught a close glimpse of Stewart some months earlier on a rowdy Christmas Eve when, together with Bill Grady and Johnny Swope, he had invaded the home of Keenan Wynn intent on sampling the Christmas liquor on Wynn's sideboard. All three were noisily inebriated and intent on becoming even more so. 'They were not the soberest trio I ever laid eyes on,' she later recalled. 'And Jimmy Stewart was not quite the Jimmy Stewart I had come to know on screen that night.'

At the Coopers' dinner party, however, he was exactly the James Stewart she had imagined – shy, awkward, stammering over the few words he did utter during dinner. Conversation was difficult. Said Gloria:

For years before I met him I read in the papers that Jimmy was Hollywood's most eligible bachelor. All sorts of rumours and gossip had been printed about his girlfriends, but I hadn't paid much attention. Nothing though had been said about him being so shy. He hardly said anything all evening. But between the pauses I could sense that the Coopers were right, that we did have a lot in common. We liked golf, sailing, animal conservation, movies of course. And I must have said something right for Jimmy took me home and the next day we had our first date – on the golf course. After that we saw each other practically every day for a year.

Gloria's main problem with James during their initial dates was getting him to part with his money. In her view he'd been a bachelor for so long he'd forgotten how to spend it. She said:

It was amazing. I had quite a time just getting him to buy me a meal. I finally had to come right out and ask him. He'd invited me to the première of the movie *You Gotta Stay Happy*. I said to him: 'If we go to this movie does it also mean that you're actually going to feed me as well?'

When faced with all this Stewart would simply pull a Jimmy Stewart expression and explain it all away by saying that he tended to be absent-minded about such things. But he later admitted:

If she says that's what happened I guess that's what did happen. Anyway, I must have loosened the rubber band around my wallet because we saw an awful lot of each other after that. Usually I took her to Dave Chasen's restaurant to eat because Bill Grady and I practically lived at the place. We had some great times there.

James and Gloria were married in Brentwood on 9 August 1949. Among the eighteen guests were Spencer Tracy, the Coopers and many of those who, the night before, had given Stewart a boisterous send off. The stag night had turned into something of a riot with Jack Benny in charge of things and a seemingly endless supply of midgets, two of whom kept popping up from inside a serving dish. The midgets were Benny's idea although he later admitted that he'd ordered rather more than he actually needed.

The stag night was held, inevitably, at Chasen's and publicized with many hastily chalked up billboards displayed outside the restaurant: 'Destry Ain't Ridin' Tonite'; 'James Stewart – Actor?'; 'Who Saw *Magic Town*?'; 'Cars Given Away'; 'Anybody Please Come'.

James and Gloria honeymooned in Honolulu before returning to make their home at a 32-year-old Tudor-style eight-bedroomed house in Beverly Hills. It was to be their home for the rest of their lives in Hollywood.

To the gossip columnists who were disappointed that Stewart hadn't chosen to marry a top Hollywood star, Stewart replied:

I've seen a lot of Hollywood marriages and the mortality rate is high. The main reason, I guess, is because both partners have their own careers and have to live apart so much … I needed the security of a permanent relationship. When you're 41 life means more than just a bookful of telephone numbers. I needed a family and to put down roots. It was the right time.

Later, when he had been married for several years, he commented: 'Hollywood being Hollywood, I guess I didn't start out with the idea of being married to one woman. I was lucky. I've nothing against actresses but it might well have been a different story if I'd gotten married to someone in the business.'

Coinciding with Stewart's new found domestic contentment came an unexpected call to make a couple of movies at his old studio MGM. The first, *Malaya*, was a routine adventure yarn that had been brought to Metro from RKO by the studio's new production head, Dore Schary. The script was uninspired and Stewart only agreed to the assignment because it allowed him to appear with Spencer Tracy, the actor who had starred in Stewart's first Hollywood movie, *Murder Man*. Later, both went on record as saying that they'd wished the reunion had been more propitious.

As it was they were stuck with a wartime yarn about smuggling rubber out of the Malay jungles in the Second World War. Stewart, as a foreign correspondent, and Tracy as a cynical adventurer, did what they could with their roles, but not even a strong supporting cast that included Lionel Barrymore, Sydney Greenstreet, Gilbert Roland and John Hodiak, could lift the proceedings above the mundane. The film's director, Richard Thorpe, wasn't exactly a plus factor. A journeyman film-maker who had the reputation of yelling 'cut-print!' after every first take, he was loathed by actors for not allowing them a second chance if a scene went badly. MGM, on the other hand, thought the world of him for bringing in all his movies under schedule.

The Stratton Story was a more gratifying affair, a real-life tale of a baseball pitcher who had been badly injured in a hunting accident, but made a remarkable comeback with an artificial leg. The story was quite mercilessly parodied by Woody Allen in his movie *Radio Days*, but back in 1949 it was just the kind of thing audiences were looking for. Stewart was brought into things after Louis B. Mayer's attempts to turn the film into a Van Johnson/June Allyson movie had come to nothing. Mayer's theory was that no picture about sport had ever made money, not even those dealing with America's favourite sport. And in that he was correct. Goldwyn had tried six years earlier with *Pride of the Yankees*, a biography of the famed Lou Gehrig. Even Gary Cooper had been unable to turn that one into a financial hit.

Mayer argued that *The Stratton Story* might just make money if they turned it into a Van Johnson/June Allyson type picture and concentrated on the personal life of Monty Stratton. 'Play down the baseball' was his edict. MGM duly began preparing the film along those lines. There had been many Johnson/Allyson movies. All of them looked alike and sounded the same, but all made money. For most at MGM, *The Stratton Story* was just another film off the conveyor belt.

It was only when Johnson had to drop out of the project that things took a turn for the better. Gregory Peck was considered for the part of Stratton but when he too failed to be available Stewart was approached, mainly because Stratton himself favoured Stewart for the role. What emerged was much more than a Van Johnson/June Allyson type movie. With Sam Wood as director and the diminutive, husky-voiced Allyson as his co-star Stewart found himself involved in a picture that was a mixture of courage, sentiment, pathos, love, despair and triumph. In many ways it was an artful concoction bringing together all the ingredients needed to make a box-office hit. Beneath the surface, however, there was still the honesty and determination of a real-life character who had managed to fight his way back to a prominent position in the game he adored.

To Stewart's surprise the film provided him with what he had been seeking since his return to film acting – a solid commercial hit. The film was MGM's biggest hit of 1949, making it the sixth highest moneymaker of the year and earning the then not inconsiderable gross of $4 million. Even L.B. was dumbfounded. When questioned about the success of *The Stratton Story* he would comment that it was the love story and the family background that really appealed to audiences, not the baseball. He even admitted that Stewart and Allyson were as good a box-office team as any he had seen on screen in the last couple of years, a fact that was borne out further when the pair teamed again in the fifties in *The Glenn Miller Story* and *Strategic Air Command*.

As 1949 drew to a close it was not surprising that in many ways Stewart was sorry to see it go. The start of a married life, an unexpected box-office hit and a return, albeit briefly, to his old studio in its twenty-fifth anniversary year, had helped make it by far the happiest year of his life. He need not have worried at its passing. The fifties were to bring even greater rewards, and they were not to be found at the mighty Metro, Paramount, Warners or any of the other top Hollywood studios, but at a studio that, as the decade drew to its close, was struggling to make ends meet and keep its head above water, Universal–International.

Footnote

1. *Saturday Evening Post* (September 1951)

11   A Rabbit and a Rifle

'If I hadn't started to make westerns I
don't think I would have survived.'
James Stewart

It was Lew Wasserman who broke the news. Stewart had
landed one of the prized screen roles of the year – the
genial eccentric Elwood P. Dowd, confidant and best
friend of the invisible 6ft rabbit, *Harvey*. It was all Stewart
could do to refrain from whooping aloud down the
telephone. Wasserman quickly tried to put things into
perspective. 'Wait a minute Jimmy. Just hold on for a
minute. There's something else.'

'Huh?'

'Universal want to do it as part of a package deal. You
have to do a western as well. Apparently its been
knocking around for some time over there and they don't
know what to do with the damn thing. If you do *Harvey*
you gotta do the western. That's the deal.'

All of which may have worried Wasserman but
concerned Stewart not one little bit. He wanted to do
Harvey so much he would quite happily have done the
western for nothing. Nonetheless, Wasserman advised
him to think about it. He understood Stewart's feelings
about *Harvey*, but a western wasn't exactly a step up the
ladder and even though other top stars were beginning to
drift back to the *genre* they were doing so in large budget
vehicles at major studios. Universal was not a major
studio, not by any stretch of the imagination. On average
it produced twenty-five pictures a year, most of them
low-budget double features.

Another drawback was that both of the movies being

offered to Stewart were to be photographed in black and white. Universal was decidedly mean about colour. On the edge financially, it preferred to reserve its use of Technicolor to enhance the beauty of Maureen O'Hara and Yvonne de Carlo. When considered in the cold light of day the package deal didn't seem so attractive after all. Wasserman advised caution but Stewart was in no mood for second thoughts. He told his agent to go ahead and agree the terms.

He had first fallen in love with the play, *Harvey*, some three years earlier, in 1947, when quite unexpectedly he had been asked to serve as a thirteen-week summer replacement for its star Frank Fay. The Broadway experience was refreshing, coming as it did so soon after the disappointment of *It's a Wonderful Life*. In fact, so enamoured did Stewart become with the play that he vowed to do his utmost to try and land the role should *Harvey* ever be adapted for the screen. When Universal purchased the rights for a million dollars he knew instinctively that he had the inside track. Frank Fay was a stage actor who had been more or less rescued from oblivion by *Harvey*. He was unknown in Hollywood. Stewart, having already scored a critical success in the play, seemed the natural choice for the film.

Lew Wasserman worked a small miracle in making the most out of what were essentially unattractive financial terms. Unimpressed with Universal's original offer he conjured up his own deal. Stewart would take only a bare minimum of 'up front' money and work for virtually no salary but once the film had been released and publicity costs deducted he would receive a percentage of the profits. Accounts of the size of the percentage varied. Some put it as high as fifty per cent, others at just ten per cent. Whatever the correct figure the deal made headlines in Hollywood. It wasn't new. Similar financial arrangements had been made in the silent days. Also at RKO in the early thirties and even at Universal itself in 1940 when the studio signed Abbott and Costello. What made it so important in 1950 was that it was the first to be hammered out in the post-war years when the studios were no longer the force they had been in the past and the star system was beginning to fall apart. The shock waves reverberated around the entire industry.

It was the western, *Winchester 73*, that went before the cameras first. A relatively simple tale it focused on one of the famous repeating rifles of 1873. Won by Stewart in a shooting contest the rifle passes from hand to hand before returning to its rightful owner. Accompanying the main storyline was a secondary Cain and Abel theme involving deceit and betrayal as Stewart searches vengefully for the brother who has murdered their father.

On the face of it the Stewart of *Winchester 73* was not unlike the Stewart of old. A bit more weathered perhaps, more laid back, a little cynical, but he was still James Stewart. At least he was for the first half of the movie. Then came a scene that caused audiences to sit bolt upright and blink in disbelief.

The scene began quietly enough in a saloon with Stewart engaging in some wary conversation with leering gunfighter Dan Duryea. When Duryea decides that Stewart is dangerous and would be better off dead, he goes for his gun. Seconds later, he is prostrate across the bar, his arm twisted savagely behind his back and his head thrust forward as Stewart, his eyes blazing and his voice quivering in uncontrollable anger, tortures him mercilessly for information. If the Universal 'deal' was a watershed so was the scene. For the first time on screen Stewart had proved that he could be as dangerous and violent – even more so – as the next man. As one critic so succinctly put it: 'It was in this film that Jimmy Stewart became James Stewart.'

The director who helped unleash all this pent-up violence was Anthony Mann. During the forties he had earned something of a reputation directing a series of low-budget *film noir* thrillers at studios that were even further down the rung than Universal. Stewart asked for him after he'd seen his work on a couple of westerns – *Devil's Doorway* which he'd made at Metro with Robert Taylor and *The Furies*, a Paramount picture with Barbara Stanwyck and Walter Huston. It turned out to be an inspired choice. Aided by the masterly camerawork of William Daniels, Mann brought to the film a stark realism and handled the action sequences with an imaginative visual flair. By rewriting, with Borden Chase, the existing screenplay he changed what had originally been an historical tale about the development of the rifle into one in which the rifle was used as an instrument to tell a story of revenge. As Mann put it:

> The gun was really a calling card for many of the characters. Every one of the characters wanted it; it was a prize. Thus you were able to meet a great many more characters because it changed hands so much. It gave the film a unity; the gun almost became a character. It brought everyone together. That's what made the film work so well.'

Stewart and Mann were lucky in that their partnership clicked from the outset. After just a few days filming they enjoyed an instant rapport. Mann said:

> I didn't know quite how we'd get on at first. You never do with actors. But once you started working with Jimmy he was marvellous because he was always there. He was always anxious; always skilful. Always co-operative. You could see he *wanted* to be great which was not exactly true of some of the other gentlemen I'd worked with.
> I suppose the funniest thing about him was that he didn't seem to realize what a great quality he had in westerns, not at first anyway. But it was obvious from my side of the camera. He was magnificent walking down a street with a Winchester rifle cradled in his arm. And he was great too when actually firing the gun. He really studied hard at it. His knuckles were raw with practising. An expert from the Winchester Arms Company taught him how to use the gun. It was these sort of things that helped make the film look so authentic and gave it its sense of reality.[1]

For his part, Stewart said that working with Mann and making *Winchester 73* turned out to be a lifesaver. He recalled:

> I know I'd really signed to do *Harvey*, but it was a huge stroke of luck that the western came along as well. If I

hadn't started to make westerns I don't think I would have survived.

I guess Tony and I were fortunate in that we were both looking for something at the same time. He was trying to make a breakthrough. I was trying to re-establish myself. Somehow, everything seemed to work out. I think maybe that we were both a little bit fortunate.

The summer of 1950 turned out to be a rewarding one for Stewart. As one critic noted, he seemed so much at ease in the saddle that he looked as though he'd been making westerns all his life. Not only did he appear in *Winchester 73* but also in a picture called *Broken Arrow*, a western he'd made at the Fox studio some twelve months earlier but which for some reason the studio were loath to put into release.

Fox's reluctance may have been because they were fearful of the consequences if it became known that the film had been scripted by the blacklisted Albert Maltz, but officially credited to Michael Blankfort. In the hysteria of the McCarthy witch-hunts the consequences for Zanuck would have been dire indeed had the facts emerged. On the other hand it may have been because the studio tended to regard the picture as not so much a western but more a social protest film of which they'd made several in the post-war years. In *The Snake Pit* they'd investigated mental illness, in *Pinky* colour prejudice, in *Gentleman's Agreement* anti-semitism. In *Broken Arrow* they looked sympathetically at the Chiricahua Apaches and revealed the Indians as people with structured lives and their own culture and set of ideals.

Whatever the reasons, however, their doubts proved to be unfounded. The film was favourably received by the critics and enjoyed financial success in the wake of *Winchester 73*. Stewart's Tom Jefords, a pioneer frontiersman who helped bring peace to the Apache nations, was not as controversial a role as that in Anthony Mann's film. There were no sudden outbursts of violence or hints of paranoia. Instead a quiet honesty in his portrait of a man who learns the dialect and customs of the Apaches as he tries to bring peace between the Indian and the white man. It was a restrained, perfectly judged performance in direct contrast to his vengeful marksman in *Winchester 73*.

It was in the midst of all this unexpected but nonetheless welcome western popularity that Stewart began to occupy himself with the film that had drawn him to Universal in the first place, *Harvey*. The studio assigned the German-born Henry Koster as director. A professional and unpretentious film-maker Koster had a deft touch with comedy and got along well with actors. In the late thirties he had been responsible for many of the Deanna Durbin vehicles that had helped save Universal from bankruptcy. With Koster, Universal felt *Harvey* was in safe hands, and so it proved. *Harvey* emerged as a film of charm and magical simplicity.

At its most basic level *Harvey* belongs with the 'funny drunk' comedies that Hollywood produced so regularly in the thirties and forties. Stewart's Elwood Dowd, an amiable but always slightly inebriated eccentric, spends most of his time conversing with his best friend – an invisible 6ft. white rabbit. Much to the embarrassment of his friends he insists on introducing Harvey to everyone he meets. His sister and her spinster daughter, with whom he lives, decide that they can stand it no longer and arrange to have him committed for treatment at a home for the mentally unstable. At the last minute, however, they decide they prefer Elwood as he is, gentle, kind, always friendly, rather than the sane man he might become if 'cured' by drugs.

For Stewart, the appeal of *Harvey* lay not in the fact that it was a comedy about an amiable drunk but because, beneath the surface, it took a wry look at the attitudes and behaviour of those who passed for normal people. It asked: 'Who is sane in this world and who isn't?' And then: 'Who is the better adjusted, Elwood or the neurotic relatives who want to cure him of his illness?'

Author Mary Chase came down firmly on the side of Elwood. In a key scene early in the film she allows him to explain his philosophy of life: 'I wrestled with reality for over thirty-five years,' he says, 'and I'm happy to say that I finally won out over it ... In this world you must be oh so smart or oh so pleasant. For years I was smart, now I recommend pleasant.'

It is a philosophy that is backed up by the down-to-earth wisdom of the cab driver who takes the uncomplaining Elwood to hospital. 'I've seen 'em before they go in and after they come out and believe me before is better. When they are cured they crab, crab, crab. They yell at me to watch the lights, watch the brakes, watch the intersection. They scream at me to hurry. Loonies are happy until they are cured.'

The critics enthused over *Harvey*. Most felt that this was one occasion when it didn't really matter whether Stewart was close to the folksy Stewart of old. His performance was both beguiling and dreamy in tone. Those who had seen Fay's original portrayal on the New York stage did carp a little, commenting that Stewart lacked some of the delicately deranged humour that Fay had brought to the part. Others welcomed the change. Stewart's Dowd they said, had a sweetness and credibility that had been lacking in Fay's portrayal.

Variety said: 'Stewart seems the perfect casting for the character so well does he convey the idea that escape from life into a pleasant half world existence has many points in its favour.' *Time* added: 'Dowd takes on the coloration of Stewart's movie personality; the gangling awkwardness, the fumbling apologetic gestures, the verbal false starts.' And *The New York Times* commented: 'Mr Stewart is disarming of all annoyance. He makes Elwood a man to be admired.'

Ironically, considering how much he had wanted to play the part, just about the only person who didn't seem all that satisfied with the performance was Stewart himself. It may have been because he was trying for perfection or that, in his mind's eye, he had an exact picture of how his screen Dowd should look and behave. Whatever it was, the end result was not what he had hoped for. 'I wasn't too satisfied with the movie,' he said later. 'I think I played him a little too dreamily. A little too cute, cute.'

The film premièred on Christmas Day, 1950. By then Universal had high expectations of Oscar success. Usually they didn't figure very much in the Oscar ceremonies.

Apart from the occasional victory in the technical categories, the awards invariably passed them by, but in 1950 both Stewart for best actor and Josephine Hull (best supporting actress for his sister) were nominated for top awards. The film itself only just missed being nominated as one of the top five pictures of the year.

In the end it was Hull and not Stewart who emerged the winner despite Louella Parsons trumpeting loudly that 'she loved *Harvey*, was going to see it again and wanted to be the first to prophecy that James Stewart would win the Academy Award.' She would have been wiser to have kept her own counsel. In her enthusiasm she overlooked the quality of the opposition: William Holden for *Sunset Boulevard*, Spencer Tracy for his harassed father of Elizabeth Taylor in *Father of the Bride*, and the eventual winner, José Ferrer for his long nosed poet-swordsman *Cyrano de Bergerac*.

Still, the movie ended yet another excellent year for Stewart, a year in which he found himself, through the success of two movies, being talked of as a rival to such veterans of the western film as John Wayne and Randolph Scott. He'd even scored a minor success in a little Fox comedy called *The Jackpot*, the story of a man whose life is drastically altered when he wins a number of big prizes in a radio competition.

Most gratifying of all was that he had helped turn the tide for Universal. In 1950 the studio went into the black for the first time in three years and mostly it was down to Stewart. Because of him other top Hollywood stars began looking in Universal's direction. The Wasserman 'deal' had also worked. When it had been agreed there were those who said that Stewart was on a hiding to nothing. That only Universal would profit from the agreement. If it had failed Stewart's future would have been bleak indeed. As it was he came out of things very nicely. For the first time since arriving in Hollywood he was on the verge of becoming one of the world's top ten money-making stars.

Footnote

1. *Screen* (July–October 1969)

12　A Clown For DeMille

'You are actors. You are being paid to do
just that – act!'

Cecil B. DeMille

No Hollywood film-maker controlled a picture as did Cecil
B. DeMille. His power was complete and absolute.

On set his customary weapon was sarcasm mixed in
with a disarming courtesy and old world charm. On some
days he would address his cast with the words 'Ladies
and Gentlemen'. On others he would be vicious,
short-tempered and contemptuous. Those who starred in
his films never forgot the experience.

James Stewart starred in just the one. The picture was
The Greatest Show on Earth, a spectacular piece of circus
hokum that also featured newcomer Charlton Heston as
the circus manager, Betty Hutton and Cornel Wilde as
rival trapeze artistes and Gloria Grahame as The Elephant
Girl. The story, such as it was, concentrated on the
everyday life and rivalries of the circus performers and
their efforts to keep their show in the black as it toured
America.

Stewart's role was the gimmick of the picture – a doctor
on the run from the police for the mercy killing of his wife.
Throughout the film he remains hidden behind a clown's
makeup. Only when a detective hands round a
photograph to members of the circus are his features seen.

Stewart was surprised to get his call-up from DeMille
but happy to accept in that his role, which was essentially
no more than a cameo, offered him something of a
breather from more rigorous assignments.

What he didn't welcome quite as much was his fee.

There were no percentages of the profits on *The Greatest Show on Earth*. Or rather there were, it was just that Stewart didn't see any of them. Paramount and DeMille divided up everything that was going.

Stewart was shaken when Lew Wasserman revealed the terms. '50,000 dollars.'

Stewart gasped, went wide-eyed and spread his hands in disbelief. 'Huh?'

'50,000 dollars,' repeated Wasserman.

'But that's insane,' said Stewart. 'I'm playing one of the key roles. I got five times that even before the Universal deal. No sir. We'll have to negotiate on this one Lew. I want what Betty Hutton's getting.'

'That's 50,000 dollars.'

'Ok, then I'll take what they're offering Cornel Wilde.'

'50,000 dollars.'

Stewart, sensing now that he was on a loser, went round all the other star names in the cast. Every time the answer was the same: 50,000 dollars. He was by no means the only one playing the 'I want more money' game. The same scene was being enacted between Cornel Wilde and his agent and between every other star and agent connected with the picture. Not one of them broke through the 50,000 dollar barrier.

DeMille's theory was that his films were seen by so many people around the world that actors should appear in them for nothing. In a way the 50,000 dollars was a bonus. Actors were lucky to get it. In their own interests it was best not to carp.

When Stewart checked this out with actors who had appeared previously for DeMille he found it had always been this way. Gary Cooper, who had starred in four of DeMille's pioneering tales of Colonial America and the Old West, told him: 'That's how it works Jimmy. Just agree the terms and play the part.'

Being directed by DeMille was an unusual experience. Even at his preliminary interview in DeMille's office Stewart was told that he was expected to come to the set word perfect and knowing exactly how he was going to play his role. 'You are actors,' DeMille told his assembled cast on the first day of shooting. 'You are being paid by me to do just that – act. If you have any problems I'll do what I can to help, but don't expect too much attention from me in that quarter. I have to save my energies for the important work. I have to take care of the crowds and the technical details.'

None of this worried Stewart unduly as he always prepared fully for every movie he made, but to some members of the cast DeMille's attitude was insulting. The effects and the photography it seemed were more important than their performances. They grumbled a lot, especially when DeMille was having one of his off-days and being mean-spirited.

For his part Stewart enjoyed watching DeMille in action almost as much as he did performing behind a clown's makeup. With his flannel shirt, well-tailored riding breeches and puttees, a huge jewelled ring on his finger and a megaphone constantly to hand the 70-year-old epic master did not disappoint. He lived up to his legend.

He was every inch the Hollywood director. Always he had three boy assistants in close attendance. One was a chairboy who never saw his master's face but was always ready with a chair to shove under DeMille's backside whenever he felt weary. Another carried a long microphone that he extended whenever DeMille needed to give instructions to the cast. A third stood ready with a tray of iced water maintained at exactly the right temperature.

No one ever referred to DeMille as 'Cecil' and only a few close friends – the writers and cameramen who had worked with him since the silent days – were allowed to call him 'CB'. A secretary was in constant attendance both in his office and when he was striding out across the Paramount lot. No one ever walked in front of him. Always, they trailed just a few steps behind. In every way he was King.

The atmosphere on the set of *The Greatest Show on Earth* was generally amicable although there were one or two who had to endure some of DeMille's merciless tongue lashing. Cornel Wilde was one. He frequently found himself at the receiving end of DeMille's sarcasm. When the director discovered that he suffered from a fear of heights and had to battle daily with his phobia DeMille was not impressed. When he saw Wilde trying on some clogs he remarked cruelly: 'Better not wear those Mr Wilde. Remember, you're afraid of heights.'

DeMille's eight assistant directors also felt the full force of DeMille's wrath. Normally, four assistant directors was the maximum number carried by a Hollywood movie, even one of epic proportions. DeMille, however, doubled up on everything to ensure that nothing went wrong. When it did and one of the film's key train sequences didn't come off as well as he had hoped he lined up the eight assistants in a quasi-military formation. Walking up and down in front of them like a Hollywood version of General Patton, he spent fully five minutes chewing them out. Never once were they allowed to speak. Not once did he repeat himself. Not once did he pause for breath. Duly chastened the assistant directors returned to their tasks. They made no more mistakes for the rest of the picture.

The tirade caused veteran members of the crew to recall other notable rows on earlier DeMille epics. On *Unconquered* for instance, when Paulette Goddard had called for a stand-in when asked to face screaming fireballs during an Indian attack. Goddard thought the request not unreasonable. She had signed on to act in the picture not to have her head blown off. DeMille was scornful. He expected courage and bravery from his stars, not cowardice. When Goddard let it be known that she was eager to land one of the roles in *The Greatest Show on Earth* DeMille refused to grant her an interview.

On *Samson and Delilah* Victor Mature was even more unfortunate. An amiable, unassuming and easy-going man, he had one serious drawback for a DeMille actor. He had a phobia about just about everything. During the filming of the biblical epic DeMille was at his most lethal. He bawled out Mature in front of the whole crew. 'Ladies and gentlemen,' said DeMille, 'I have met a few men in my time. Some have been afraid of heights, some have been afraid of open spaces, some even of themselves. But, in all my years of picture-making experience Mr Mature I have not, until now, met a man who was one hundred per cent yellow.'

The incident that precipitated the outburst was when Mature baulked at having to do a scene in which an actor playing a giant Philistine lashed out with a whip and coiled it around Mature's waist. The actor was a 6ft. 5in., 18st. wrestler who went by the name of 'Wee Willie'. He needed to be deadly accurate from twenty yards. Mature, not unreasonably, felt that it might be a good idea if he retired to his dressing room and a double was used in his stead.

DeMille strode scornfully onto the set and instructed 'Wee Willie' to aim at him and crack the whip. The director, protected only by his shirt, caught the whip as it coiled viciously around his waist and pulled the actor towards him. He snapped at Mature: 'That's what I expect you to do. *That's* what I'm paying you for!'

During the filming of *The Greatest Show on Earth* Stewart also witnessed the other side of DeMille, the patient, courteous and kindly side. It occurred in a scene in which an extra was required to rush up to Charlton Heston and utter the line: 'Hey, Brad, Holly's spinnin' like a weathervane in a Kansas twister.' It was by no means an easy line, and the ageing bit player, who had been a member of DeMille's stock company for many years, couldn't get it right. He muffed twenty-seven straight takes. After two hours of patient cajoling he was still fluffing. DeMille had no alternative but to have him replaced. The crew were silent and embarrassed, but they had respect for DeMille that day. He never lost his temper once.

The Greatest Show on Earth was described by many as 'the circus movie to end all circus movies'. A number of critics lashed out, as they frequently did when faced with a DeMille picture, calling it a piece of 'super kitsch' and 'run of DeMille'.

DeMille though was used to such taunts, and had the last laugh when the film surprised everyone (DeMille included if truth be known) by winning the Oscar as the best picture of 1952. Stewart's role as the sad clown with the dark past was strictly a minor performance, but he made his character genuinely appealing and the long hours he spent with the great American clown Emmett

Kelly who had a small role in the picture were among the happiest he'd ever spent on a movie set.

By the time he'd finally wiped away the last of DeMille's greasepaint Stewart was coming to terms with the very pleasant fact that he was to become the father of twins. Gloria had broken the news to him a few months earlier when he had been filming in England on the film version of Nevil Shute's bestseller *No Highway*. The news brightened his mood considerably as he set about creating Shute's absent-minded British boffin who warns his bosses that unless all airliners that have flown more than 1,440 miles are grounded immediately they will crash because of metal fatigue. Sadly the film didn't live up to its potential. Despite a reteaming with Marlene Dietrich (as a film star trapped on one of the doomed planes) there was little to recommend it other than a variation on Stewart's Elwood P. Dowd performance in *Harvey*, a performance Gloria had discovered that was not so very far removed from the real-life Jimmy Stewart she had known for three years.

By 1952 she had become accustomed to all of his mannerisms – his hesitancy, his slow manner of speaking, his relaxed 'I haven't a care in the world' way of doing things. All that is except one: his absent-mindedness. Leland Hayward had warned her many times that she would never be able to rely on him to turn up on time and that he would simply forget where he was supposed to be and at what time. He would cite an occasion in New York when Stewart had forgotten to fill his wallet with that most vital of commodities – cash. Hayward recalled:

We had to take a lot of taxis and naturally, I paid. We went to a restaurant. Again, I paid. It was the same with the hatcheck girl. Then he borrowed some money to make some telephone calls. When I had to dig in my pocket to buy his newspaper I finally blew my top. 'Don't you *ever* carry money?' I yelled.

I could see that I had really upset him. He looked real unhappy and reached into his pocket. Out came a dried-up, shrivelled banana. I burst out laughing. The next day he sent me a gift – a hand tooled leather wallet that obviously had cost him twenty times the money I'd spent. How could anyone possibly be angry with such a guy?[1]

Stewart himself has never made any excuses for his absent-mindedness: 'I know I'm a dreamer. Always have been. I'm very guilty of day dreaming. I just can't seem to keep my mind on one idea – that's why I don't read much, just film scripts.' He also admits to being the world's worst driver:

> Gloria would never allow the children in the car when I was driving. I was a terrible driver. Still am. I don't seem to be able to concentrate. I have this terror that I will drive into something one day. Lots of times I have felt grateful to drive into my garage at home. Driving has always been something of an ordeal for me.

The real test of his driving skills (or the lack of them) occurred as the birth of the twins drew near. Gloria viewed James's meticulous planning with some apprehension, especially when he began making trial runs to the Cedars of Lebanon Hospital where she had a room booked. He even began timing himself with a stop-watch until he got lost and had to ask at a gas station where he was.

As things turned out all the planning came to nothing for Gloria was taken into hospital early, suffered complications and, after a Caesarean operation, gave birth to two healthy girls, Judy and Kelly. Gloria said:

> I was in hospital a long time before they said I could go home and when I was finally allowed to leave I realized that Jimmy's meticulous planning would come into effect in reverse. And that didn't exactly fill me with confidence.
>
> Anyway, he came to the hospital to help move me and my luggage and all the flower pots I'd accumulated. I was in a wheelchair. Jim said: 'I'll go down and get the car out of the garage and bring it round to the ambulance entrance. You go down in the elevator and I'll meet you there.'
>
> I went down all right, but Jim forgot to pick me up. He just got into his car and went home. Twenty minutes

passed and the nurse asked, 'Where could he be?' Knowing the man, I said calmly: 'He's forgotten.' She protested. 'He *couldn't* have forgotten.' I said: 'Take me back upstairs, he'll phone.' We went back and sure enough, the phone rang.

Jim had started home and stopped at a photographer's studio to pick up some pictures. The photographer asked: 'How is Mrs Stewart?' Then he ran to the phone, called me and said: 'I'll be right down.' He hadn't forgotten the babies because by that time they'd been home a month. He'd just forgotten me.

Stewart's frequent bewilderment at all the comings and goings, the traumas and delights of becoming a father of twins in no way made him forget the professional side of his life. In between helping to feed the babies and enjoying a domestic bliss he had never before known, he kept in touch with Universal. The studio were anxious to reactivate his partnership with Anthony Mann and to capitalize on the success of *Winchester 73*. Another western was what they wanted. And it was Stewart who was responsible for supplying the story when a friend recommended a novel called *Bend of the River*. Stewart suggested it to Universal because he liked the novel's cover. Universal also liked what was between the covers and purchased the screen rights.

On 25 June Stewart bade a temporary farewell to his family in Brentwood and headed for the rough terrains of Oregon and the Snake River. This time Universal did not stint. The budget was doubled and Technicolor used. The Mann-Stewart relationship that was to prosper and keep Stewart among the top money-making stars for the rest of the decade had begun in earnest.

Footnote

1. *Everybody's Man*, Jhan Robbins, Robson Books (1985)

13   The Westerns of Anthony Mann

'He could be extremely volatile. When he snapped the danger would come on very strong.'

Clint Eastwood

Stewart's willingness to perform many of his own stunts made him a popular actor when filming westerns. The really dangerous stuff he left to the stuntmen, but whenever there was something within his compass – a fight scene, a tricky riding sequence – he would frequently volunteer his services. It was one of the things director Anthony Mann most admired about him and that helped keep them together for eight movies over a period of five years.

It was the last of these films, *The Man From Laramie*, that provided Stewart with his most hazardous sequence. The scene was set on a wide expanse of salt flats some hundred miles north of Santa Fe. It called for Stewart to be taunted by a wild gang of unruly ranch-hands, lassoed and then pulled headfirst through a camp fire. The scene was set for a noon shoot under a scorching New Mexico sun.

Normally, Mann agreed to Stewart's suggestions knowing full well that none of the star's physical efforts would be likely to do him any harm. This was different, however. There were obvious dangers even though the scene itself would take only a few seconds to film. Stewart could get burned. His eyes could be damaged and his face scorched. Even a minor injury could delay the already tight twenty-eight-day shooting schedule. The film was being produced by Harry Cohn's Columbia studio. Cohn was not a man who took kindly to his movies running over budget. If something went wrong Mann knew that he would be the one who would carry the can and have to face the Columbia boss. He decided not to risk it. 'Too dangerous Jimmy,' he told the actor. 'We'll use a double.'

Stewart was not to be put off so easily.

'You know it'll look better if I do it Tony,' he argued. 'There's no need for a stunt double on this. It's a short scene. And you'll be able to use close-ups. I'm not going to die. It's only a small camp fire.'

'Yeah, but if you get burned or …'

'I won't, I won't,' Stewart waved his hand at the cameraman and yelled: 'Let's do it!'

Mann shrugged. He knew better than to argue the point. Stewart could be stubborn. When he got the bit between his teeth there was little one could do to persuade him otherwise. In any case he would rather Stewart do the scene anyway. It was just the thought of Harry Cohn's temper that kept niggling away at the back of his mind. Thirty minutes later, with the camera set up and the Columbia crew at the ready, Mann called 'Action'.

Alex Nicol, the actor playing the leading bad guy, circled on horseback and yelled at his men. 'Let's see how good you can use that rope,' he cried at one of them. Stewart, on foot and unsure of which way to turn, was unable to avoid the lasso. Struggling to free himself, he stumbled and then plunged headfirst into the fire, emerging with his face blackened and wiping the dust from his eyes as he struggled to his feet.

'Jerk him down if he needs it,' yelled Nicol. 'Now burn the wagons.' Seconds later the wagons were alight and Stewart's mules being brutally slaughtered. A scene of civilized tranquillity had turned into one of sadistic savagery in just ninety seconds. 'Cut,' cried Mann, 'and print!'

There was just the one take. No reshoots were necessary. There had been no need for a stuntman. The movie was still on schedule. An hour later the unit moved on to the next location as it continued its 2,000 mile trek around the Santa Fe area. The movie came in on time. There was no need to worry about Harry Cohn.

The key to the success of the Stewart-Mann partnership was that both men admired and enjoyed the western.

Unlike other stars and directors who regarded it as just another way of fulfilling a studio contract, Stewart and Mann saw it as an important film *genre* – uniquely American and perfect for telling primitive and often very violent tales against the most striking of settings. There were no rules or limitations with the western. In the view of both men, just about any story could be set in the West.

For Mann, it was the landscapes that were the main attraction. For his cavalry westerns John Ford went for the splendours of Monument Valley. Mann, on the other hand, sought out more rugged terrain. Canyons and snow-capped mountains and desolate plains were the settings for his tales. The stark contrasts of his landscapes enhanced the power of his stories. His visual flair was always in evidence. 'Always use the scenery to the best effect,' he said. 'Never go indoors unless you have to. Scenery enhances everything. It enhances the story; it enhances the action and the acting. I never show a piece of scenery, a gorge, a chasm, without an actor in it somewhere. The scenery is there. Use it!'

For his part, Stewart tended to accept the films more at face value. In his view the western was a traditional movie entertainment that had not been fully explored. He saw his heroes as vulnerable men. They may have been wounded or scarred by something in their past, but they triumphed over their adversity. He later recalled: 'In those films I guess I was the plodder, the inarticulate man who tried. I was a pretty good example of human frailty. But for some reason I made it. Somehow, I got through. When I was at the head of the wagon train we got across the water.'

Stewart's forte in the Anthony Mann films was the cynical loner, an embittered man looking for a new life, but at the same time seeking out the man or men who have wronged him. His westerners were all extensions of his Lin McAdam in *Winchester 73*, lean, laconic men with an air of edginess about them. At times they were almost schizophrenic figures, men of vengeance, driven by obsession and embittered by failure and defeat.

A young actor who was much impressed and later influenced by Stewart's portrayals for Anthony Mann was the 24-year-old Clint Eastwood. In the early fifties he had just signed with Universal and was embarking on a career in the studio's double features. Sometimes he would watch Stewart in action on the lot. On other occasions he would see his movies at the studio's preview theatre. The Stewart he watched in those days left a lasting impression:

> He had a great way with violence. Most people don't realize that about him but when he was mad about something, when he had been wronged in a film, when he showed anger, it was much more intense than in most actors. He could be extremely volatile. When he snapped the danger would come on very strong. It always stayed with me.[1]

Stewart and Mann collaborated on four westerns between 1952 and 1955. In the first, Universal's *Bend of the River*, Stewart was a former Missouri border raider who teams up with horse thief Arthur Kennedy and guides some fruit farmers to Oregon. Later, over at Metro, he starred in *The Naked Spur*, this time as a neurotic bounty hunter desperate for the $5,000 reward needed to help him regain the land he has lost in the Civil War. Back at Universal in *The Far Country* he appeared as a hard-bitten wrangler forced to avenge the death of his longtime partner Walter Brennan.

It was *The Man From Laramie*, however, that remained Stewart's favourite of the quartet. In many ways it was a rehash of many of the elements of the earlier films, a tough, violent tale about an army captain seeking out those responsible for the death of his younger brother, a Cavalry officer killed by Apaches armed with automatic rifles. Once again, the revenge motive was in evidence, and once again the exteriors were strikingly photographed, but on this occasion Mann added an extra ingredient, a touch of sadism, as he showed the terrible effects of a bullet fired at a human from close range.

The scene occurred in the latter stages of the film when Stewart once again finds himself surrounded by Alex Nicol's minions. Held from behind and kicking and grunting as he realizes the violence that is about to be perpetrated on him, he gasps for breath as his arm is held firm and the leather glove pulled from his hand. Nicol holds the gun just six inches from the naked palm. Stewart, struggling, widens his eyes in terror. As the gun fires the camera cuts again to Stewart's face. Uttering a girlish shriek and barely conscious he squeals at Nicol: 'You scum' then stumbles away from the camera holding his hand. One of the cowhands helps him onto his horse. Slumped over the saddle he rides slowly away from the camera and into the distance.

Rarely if ever had the cinema of the West indulged in such a sadistic act; rarely had Stewart been more effective in a scene. It remains one of his most arresting pieces of acting.

Stewart's total effectiveness in westerns was put down by Mann to his believability. He said:

> That's what people liked about him. They seemed to sense that he belonged out West. They never got the feeling that, oh, this was an actor playing at westerns. They felt he belonged there. He was always a bit grubby, dirty even and looking as though he could use a drink or a square meal.
>
> A battered sheepskin jacket, stubble on his chin, riding off for some confrontation in the high country – it was all part of Jimmy Stewart.
>
> Most of all he seemed to have something more burning and exciting on screen than when you met him personally. That always came across on screen. And his emotion when roused was something we concentrated on of course, especially after *Winchester 73*.

Stewart's screen anger was never more vividly demonstrated than in *Bend of the River*. Badly beaten and betrayed by his former partner, Arthur Kennedy, he is left abandoned on Mount Hood without either a horse or a gun. In a quivering voice and eyes filled with hate he tells Kennedy that he should have killed him when he had the chance. 'You'll be seeing me,' he cries. 'Every time you look back in the darkness and bed down for the night you'll wonder if I'm there. One night I will be. You'll be seeing me!'

Kennedy's triumphant smirk as he leers down from his horse gradually fades to be replaced by one of apprehension, and little wonder. This Stewart was about as far removed from the idealistic Mr Smith of Washington or George Bailey of Bedford Falls as it was possible to get.

The success of the Stewart-Mann partnership was put down to many things – that both men were roughly the same age (the mid forties), that they shared the same professional approach to movie-making and that they admired the screenplays of their regular writers Borden Chase and Philip Yordan. On a minor level, however, there was another reason. Stewart wore the same hat and rode the same horse in every western he made with the director. Since *Winchester 73* he had developed into a highly superstitious actor about both hat and horse. To make sure his hat wouldn't get lost in a studio property room or be loaned out to some other actor he had it locked in a vault for safekeeping. Mann said:

> You wouldn't believe the trouble we had getting that hat. It took us something like two months to get the right one for Jimmy. It's a funny thing about hats. People tend to take them for granted. But getting the right hat is one of the most important things about making westerns because it's very rarely taken off. If you don't get the right hat you might as well not get on a horse.
>
> John Wayne was a big man and could wear a big hat. Jimmy was very slim and couldn't. Some of the tests we made were hysterical. We eventually got him a hat full of holes and with a big greasy sweatband. I remember the hat got a great notice in *The New York Times*.[2]

Stewart first became acquainted with his horse, Pie, during the filming of *Winchester 73*. He was an accomplished rider having learned as a boy on the horse that used to be tethered behind his father's hardware store. When it became apparent, however, that he was going to have to do some serious riding in front of the cameras he knew he would have to find the right horse. Universal suggested he checked out the horses of Stevie Myers, the daughter of Roy Myers who had supplied horses for Tom Mix, Gene Autry and other western stars. Stewart said:

> She brought out five or six horses. They were all big, sloppy things that moseyed around. Then I saw this horse peeking around the corner of a barn. I said: 'Who's that?'
> She said: 'That's my horse.'
> And I said: 'Well, could I just get on him?'
> She said: 'Sure, you can ride him but I usually don't give him to anyone else because he's thrown about five guys and he doesn't have a very good reputation. But if you like him ...'
> Well, I just fell in love with the horse. I had him for twenty years. Whenever there was a chance to mention him by name in a movie I did so. He was a wonderful horse. Never known another like him.
> When he got older, I'd see him with a lot of younger horses which were trained to do various things for the cameras. But they'd sort of sit around ... Pie, whenever he had to go out on a dead run, he didn't like to be in the pack. He liked to be in front, whether we were supposed to be or not. Wonderful horse, wonderful. I never owned him. Stevie wouldn't sell but she always made him available whenever I wanted him for a movie.[3]

It wasn't only westerns that occupied Stewart and Mann in the early fifties. Both men so enjoyed working with each other that they happily accepted other assignments from other studios. Just about all of the major companies tried to jump on the bandwagon so sure were they that star and director equated with box-office success.

Even Universal, stuck for a new western story, came up with an adventure tale about oil rigs in Louisiana. Stewart played an oil driller up against the fishermen of the area. The film was called *Thunder Bay*.

Said Mann: 'We tried but it was all too fabricated and the story was weak. We were never able to lick it. But they wanted a Jimmy Stewart picture so we concocted one. It was as simple as that. It didn't get terribly good notices but of course it made a profit.'

It was the same story over at Paramount. There the pair joined forces for a flag-waving exercise called *Strategic Air Command*. Stewart was active in the Voluntary Air Reserve and was happy to make the picture even though its story was so thin as to be non-existent. The plot, such as it was, dealt with a successful baseball player who is recalled to the Air Force to help operate the B-36s and B-47s, then 'the biggest single factor in the security of the world'. Eventually, realizing the importance of the work, he renounces baseball to serve as a full-time officer. Stewart played the pilot, June Allyson was once again his wife and William Daniels helped contribute some outstanding Technicolor camerawork. The result of all the endeavours was a huge box-office gross of $6.5 million.

Even more successful was yet another Universal project, *The Glenn Miller Story*. This cast Stewart as the legendary trombonist who spent most of the thirties searching for an elusive new sound before becoming one of the most successful band leaders of all time.

Nowadays, the film is regarded as one of the great popular classics of the period, but at the time of its production it was something of a gamble. Bio-pics of entertainers and band leaders had not fared too well in the post-war years. One had to go back to *The Jolson Story*, made eight years earlier, to find a hit movie based on the life of an entertainer, and that had only been made because Columbia's Harry Cohn had said yes when every other studio in town had said no.

United Artists had come up against the other side of the coin when they'd tried to capitalize on the popularity of the two Dorsey bands in their 1946 production, *The Fabulous Dorseys*. They even went so far as to cast Tommy and Jimmy Dorsey as themselves. All to no avail. The public wanted to hear the Dorseys on disc and in the dance halls. They did not want to watch their life story on film. *The Fabulous Dorseys* laid an egg.

The news therefore that Universal were planning a major movie on the life of Glenn Miller took Hollywood by surprise. Miller had been dead for ten years and although his music was still popular his life had not been a long one. He was just forty when the plane that was carrying him from London to Paris was reported missing whilst crossing a foggy English Channel in December 1944.

Universal though calculated shrewdly. Stewart was their trump card for he was now number four at the box office. Only John Wayne, Martin and Lewis and Gary Cooper were ahead of him in the list of the world's top money-making stars. Casting June Allyson once more as his wife was another plus. Then there was the music itself. Universal brought together every hit tune Miller had recorded, highlighting the most popular in key sequences and featuring the others as background music to accompany Miller's rise to fame. They also threw in a wonderful jam session at Basin Street with Louis Armstrong, Gene Krupa and other jazz greats. They then rounded the whole thing off with one of the biggest tearjerking climaxes in movie history with June Allyson sobbing uncontrollably as she hears of her husband's death and listens to 'Little Brown Jug' coming over the radio.

If Allyson wept buckets audiences wept even more. They loved every minute. Sentimental and stimulating by turn, the film was a hit from the very first day of its release.

That its success was largely down to Stewart was clearly demonstrated two years later when Universal tried to repeat their success with *The Benny Goodman Story*. This time there was no Stewart and no June Allyson. Instead there was Steve Allen and Donna Reed. Anthony Mann did not direct. The film failed.

In view of their remarkable success together it was ironic that the Stewart-Mann partnership finally came to an end on an unhappy note. Things finished because of a disagreement.

Stewart had wanted them to get together again on another western called *Night Passage*. Stewart had agreed to the project. Mann had indicated that he was mildly interested. The film was the tale of a railroad cop (Stewart) whose younger brother (played by Audie Murphy) belongs to an outlaw gang led by Dan Duryea. The teaming of Stewart and Murphy was intriguing but Mann eventually decided that the film was no more than a formula oater and backed off. He pronounced the story as being too weak and opted instead for a tougher, more realistic western at Paramount, *The Tin Star*, starring Henry Fonda. Stewart was upset about Mann's withdrawal. The two men parted company. They never worked together again. Mann, especially, regretted it.

As things turned out, Mann was proved right about *Night Passage*. The film was released in 1957. It was directed by James Neilson and it flopped. Stewart didn't make another western for five years.

Footnotes

1. *James Stewart: A Wonderful Life*, Educational Broadcasting Corporation (1987)
2. *Screen* (July–October 1969)
3. *Film Comment* (March–April 1990)

14   Three for Hitch!

'Grace had that twinkle and a touch of
larceny in her eye.'

James Stewart

In 1954 Alfred Hitchcock once again sought the services of
James Stewart.

'Have you got a good story?' the actor asked.

'I've got a good *short* story,' said Hitch and went on to
describe a Cornell Woolrich tale about a news photographer who is confined to a wheelchair with a broken leg.
Unable to move from his Greenwich Village apartment he
believes a murder has been committed in the apartment
opposite. With the help of his glamorous, socialite
girlfriend, his down-to-earth masseuse and an old
detective friend he eventually traps the killer. Never once
does he move out of his apartment. The story was called
Rear Window.

At first Stewart didn't respond to the idea since the last
occasion he and Hitch had worked together had been on
the one set fiasco, *Rope*. Now it seemed that Hitchcock was
once again dipping his toes into similarly dangerous
waters – one set, a New York setting, no room to move the
camera and formidable technical problems. Once Hitch
had guaranteed that there would be no dolly or tracking
shots and certainly no ten-minute takes, however, he was
reassured. Hitchcock in 1954 was a very different director
to the one he'd been in the late forties. With such hits as
the ingenious swap-murder thriller *Strangers on a Train* to
his credit, he was firmly back in his stride, full of his old
confidence and eager to tackle the problems the film
posed.

He also made the film doubly attractive to Stewart by casting the cool 25-year-old blonde Grace Kelly as his leading lady. Kelly was just beginning to make an impact in Hollywood. As Gary Cooper's Quaker bride in *High Noon* and the repressed safari wife enamoured with Clark Gable in *Mogambo* she had shown unmistakeable signs of star potential. Hitchcock further enhanced her stature by signing her for his film version of the stage thriller, *Dial M For Murder*. The critics were impressed, not only with her looks but by her acting ability.

Her *Dial M* co-star Ray Milland found her irresistible. Nearly twice Kelly's age at forty-eight, and with a wife and family at home, he went into a tailspin over the actress, embarking on an affair that became the talk of Hollywood. When Milland prepared to move out to set up home with Kelly the gossip columnists lit up with the news that Milland's wife was going to sue for divorce. Milland was prepared for the outcome, Kelly was not. When faced with life with the suave Ray and the accompanying scandal that could ruin her career she dropped him like a hot potato.

The affair helped add fuel to the rumour that, as far as men were concerned, Grace was something of a predator in Hollywood. The French actor Jean-Pierre Aumont, Bill Holden and Clark Gable had all been seduced by her charms (although in Gable's case he insisted it was his idea) and there was inevitable talk that James Stewart might be next on the list.

By 1954, however, Stewart had been married for five years, was a father of four and as happily married as any Hollywood actor could expect to be. He had no desire to become romantically involved with any of his leading ladies. There had been a time when things might have been different, but that was in the dim and distant past. He did make a point of sending Kelly flowers on occasion, but that was just his old-style gentlemanly way of going about things.

For her part, Gloria was fully aware of the Milland affair and the teasing quality Kelly possessed that made men lose their heads over her. She kept her silence at the time, but later confessed that there were times when she had been worried. She said:

Jimmy was working with some of the most glamorous women in the world during that period. My constant fear I suppose was that he would find them more attractive than me and have an affair with one of them.

A lot of men in Hollywood constantly became involved with their leading ladies. Jimmy was a red blooded American male so naturally I thought it could happen to him too. I was convinced that it would only be a matter of time before the phone would ring and it would be James telling me he had to work late at the studio or that he would be out playing poker with the boys.

Well, no such phone call ever came. And I can honestly say that in all the years we'd been married Jimmy never once gave me cause for anxiety or jealousy. The more glamorous the leading lady he was starring opposite, the more attentive he'd be to me.

Grace Kelly was certainly glamorous in *Rear Window*. She'd never looked so stunning. Gowned by Paramount's top costume designer, Edith Head, she gave off more erotic power than any Hitchcock actress since Ingrid Bergman. The only major criticism that was levelled against her was that she was cold. It was not an opinion with which Stewart agreed. He said:

She was anything but cold. Everything about Grace was appealing. I was married but I wasn't dead. She had those big warm eyes and well, if you had ever played a love scene with her, you'd know she wasn't cold. She had an inner confidence. People who have that are not cold. Grace had that twinkle and a touch of larceny in her eye.

Everyone – director, stars, technicians – sensed they were on to a winner with *Rear Window*. The atmosphere on set was always on a high, the mood buoyant and confident. Hitch's enthusiasm and the way he battled to solve his technical problems was contagious. His gigantic Greenwich Village set was his own personal toy. It occupied one entire sound stage on the Paramount lot and had been built for him by art directors Hal Pereira and Joseph McMillan Johnson. It included no less than thirty-one apartments, most of which could be seen in some form by Stewart from the vantage point of his room.

Twelve of the apartments, including those of a struggling composer, a lonely spinster, a ballet student and the suspected wife murderer, were completely furnished even though they were always viewed in long shot. Whenever visitors dropped by at the studio Hitch insisted that they called in on his *Rear Window* set where he would explain with pride the intricacies of his production. His constant enthusiasm for his project meant that he was amiable company on set. He relished the raunchy jokes he delivered daily. His humour was earthy and vulgar. He thought it would shock Grace Kelly. It didn't. She replied with a cool smile: 'I went to a girl's convent school Mr Hitchcock. I heard all those things when I was thirteen.'

He also delighted in taunting both Stewart and Kelly with his much quoted remark 'Actors are like cattle'. When Stewart challenged him on this Hitchcock proved his point in the simplest of ways. He shot a close-up of Stewart smiling and then cut immediately to a shot of a toddler waddling up a path. Result: Stewart, a kindly father.

Next, Hitch used exactly the same close-up of Stewart, but this time cut it together with a shot of a bikini clad pin-up girl. Result: Stewart, a dirty old man. 'Putty in my hands', Hitch would say to Stewart, Kelly and the rest. With such evidence placed before them it was difficult for anyone to argue much of a case after that.

As to the charge that Hitchcock rarely gave much direction to his actors, Thelma Ritter perhaps summed it up best in her characteristically down-to-earth way. She played Stewart's visiting masseuse in the movie. 'You knew whether you were OK or not,' she said. 'If he liked what you did he said nothing. If he didn't he looked as though he was going to throw up!'

Critics hailed *Rear Window* as by far the best of Hitchcock's post-war efforts. Some went so far as to say that it was the best he had ever made. The public agreed. They paid out more than $6 million to view not only the brilliantly sustained suspense, but also the on-screen chemistry that existed between Stewart and Kelly. Just prior to its release the trade paper *Variety* accurately summed up its potential in the market place:

> Hitchcock combines technical and artistic skills in a manner that makes this an unusually good piece of murder-mystery entertainment. There's a very earthy quality to the relationship between Stewart and Miss Kelly. She's a Park Avenue girl not above using her physical charms to convince Stewart they should get married. This is carried to the point where she arrives one evening to spend the night and gives him what she calmly calls 'a preview of coming attractions' by donning a frilly nightgown and négligé. Both do a fine job of the picture's acting demands.

The only qualm voiced by some critics was that *Rear Window* was something of an immoral picture. Stewart, plus the audience, were acting as peeping toms, peeking in on the private lives of people who were unaware of being watched. C.A. Lejeune of the London *Observer* was especially vehement. She called *Rear Window* a horrible picture and added that the hero was nothing more than a snooper.

To which Hitchcock replied: 'That's nonsense. Nine out of ten people, if they see a woman across a courtyard undressing for bed or even a man pottering around in his room, will stay and look; no one turns away and says its none of my business. They could pull their blinds but never do; they stand there and look out.'

Paramount's reaction to the success of *Rear Window* was the same as Universal's over the success of the Anthony Mann westerns: 'Let's have another Jimmy Stewart/Alfred Hitchcock picture – and as soon as possible.' As soon as possible turned out to be some two years later, in 1956, when star and director were eventually reunited for *The Man Who Knew Too Much*. By then Stewart had completed his films with Anthony Mann and Hitch had made the third and last of his films with Kelly, *To Catch A Thief*.

The Man Who Knew Too Much was a thriller that Hitch had already made in Britain in the thirties – a tight, intriguing picture involving a kidnap plot and an attempted assassination in London. In 1934 the film had run to just eighty-four minutes; in the 1956 remake, with VistaVision and Technicolor as added ingredients, it ran for some two hours. Instead of using Swiss locations as he had done in the first movie, Hitch opted for the more exotic locale of Morocco.

Stewart's role was that of an American doctor holidaying with his wife and son in North Africa. When he learns of an assassination due to take place during a concert at the Albert Hall, his son is kidnapped to ensure his silence. It was all very unlikely and wildly over melodramatic, but Stewart was perfectly at home in his usual Hitchcock role of Mr Everyman thrown into a bizarre and dangerous situation and carrying the audience with him as he tries to come to terms with events previously outside his experience.

Whether Hitch would have chosen Grace Kelly for the role of Stewart's wife is debatable. It was hardly her kind of role and in any case the whole thing was academic anyway. Grace Kelly had by then retired from acting to become Princess Grace of Monaco.

Even so, his choice of Doris Day caused more than a few raised eyebrows. The part required her to work her way through the whole gamut of emotion. Smiles and apple-pie order were what were needed in the film's opening scenes; anguish, hysteria, tears and panic were the prime ingredients of the remaining ninety minutes. And in the middle of all this she was required to render two versions of a Jay Livingston–Ray Evans song called 'Que Sera, Sera'.

By now Stewart knew Hitchcock as well as he knew Anthony Mann. He was perfectly at ease with the director's methods. To stars new to the director he would advise: 'We're in the hands of an expert. You can lean on him. Just do everything he tells you and the whole thing will be OK.'

Doris Day, however, was distinctly ill-at-ease during filming. She had never before left the States and the picture required a great deal of travel, not only to Morocco, but also in London. She was upset by the strange food and the lack of hygiene in Marrakesh.

Hitchcock's detached approach also disturbed her. He never praised or criticised. He just called 'cut' and prepared for the next set-up. By the time they got to London she was convinced that he was deeply unhappy with her acting.

When she confided her fears to Stewart he passed them on to Hitch. Hitch was amazed. Everything was perfect, he said. If they hadn't been he would have told her so. He further reassured her that he knew she could act. He'd seen her some six years earlier in a dramatic film she'd made for Warners called *Storm Warning*. The film had been a tough tale about the activities of the Ku Klux Klan. Ever since he'd seen that film he never had any doubts about her acting abilities. From that moment on Doris Day had no acting problems on *The Man Who Knew Too Much*.

Stewart relished the sight of Hitch at work in Morocco. He was especially amused at the way he handled some annoying crowd problems. He said:

I remember that the temperature was in the 100s with the native Arabs churning around. Someone evidently had told the people who had been hired as background extras that if they weren't in a position where they could see the camera they wouldn't be paid. The assistant directors would put the people where they were supposed to be, but as soon as a signal for a take was given they'd all turn and stare at the camera!

It was chaos but Hitch was never bothered. Throughout all the misunderstandings and the heat, with everyone in their shirt sleeves and sweat on their brow, Hitch was right down in the centre of things in a blue suit with a collar and tie in place. He sat in a chair which had a big umbrella hooked to it. He was never seen without his jacket. The heat never seemed to bother him.

Compared with *Rear Window*, *The Man Who Knew Too Much* was strictly a routine spy adventure, entertaining in its formularized way and climaxed by a brilliantly edited assassination attempt at the Albert Hall. Everyone gave a good account of themselves, from Stewart and Day to the supporting actors, many of whom played spies – the French performer Daniel Gelin, Britain's Bernard Miles and Brenda de Banzie and, as the Albert Hall assassin, Reggie Nalder. It was basically 'in between' stuff, however, something to make money and a prelude to a darker much more sombre tale that Hitchcock had been preparing for some time.

The film was called *Vertigo* and was based on the Pierre Boileau and Thomas Narcejac novel *From Among The Dead*. More a portrait of obsession than a mechanical thriller it offered Stewart his most demanding Hitchcock role, that of a San Francisco police detective who is retired from the force when his fear of heights causes the death of a fellow policeman. When a former college friend asks him to take on a private job and trail his beautiful blonde wife, Stewart finds himself becoming obsessed with the woman. He rescues her from a suicide attempt in San Francisco bay but, because of his phobia, is later powerless to prevent her death from a fall from a bell tower. When he meets her double his all-consuming obsession returns and he insists on recreating down to the last detail, the woman he has loved and lost.

Two thirds of the way through the film both Stewart and the audience learn that the two women are one and the same and that Stewart has been set up in a complex murder plot. In the end fate decrees that the woman shall die again, from the same bell tower.

For Stewart it was the terror that could come from the fear of heights that appealed to him. He said:

> I had known fear like that and I'd known people who'd been paralyzed by fear. It's a very powerful thing to be almost engulfed by that kind of fear. I didn't realize when I was preparing for the role what an impact it would have but it was an extraordinary achievement by Hitch. And I could tell it was a very personal film for him even while he was making it.'

It was also a very difficult film with casting and script as the main problems. Stewart was no trouble. He was automatic. It was the leading lady, who essentially had to play two parts, that created the real headache.

At first Hitchcock settled on Vera Miles. He had used her effectively a year before as the wife of Henry Fonda in

The Wrong Man and would do so again two years later in *Psycho*. She wasn't exactly a substitute for the glamorous Grace Kelly but she was an accomplished performer and Hitch knew that she would be able to handle the film's later, more difficult scenes. He did not know however that she would become pregnant shortly before the film's start date and have to withdraw at the last moment.

The withdrawal threw him into a state of confusion mainly because there seemed to be no obvious replacement. Doris Day was obviously unsuited to the part and it was with some reluctance that he accepted Kim Novak who had then risen to become one of the top box-office stars in the country. The argument was that since *Vertigo* was not as obviously commercial as the earlier Stewart/Hitchcock collaborations, Novak's presence would at least offer box-office insurance.

Hitchcock's temper was not improved by the fact that he could secure her services only by promising that Stewart would make a comedy for Columbia the following year. His state of mind was improved even less when, early in 1957, he fell ill and had to be hospitalized because of a diseased gall bladder. Almost the last straw was when his screenwriter Alec Coppel who had been labouring for months on the script, delivered an uninspired screenplay that did little justice to the story.

Hitchcock's immediate reaction to the catalogue of misfortune was to say enough's enough and cancel the production, but he made one last throw. He asked playwright Samuel Taylor, a native of San Francisco, to have a crack at the story. Taylor cut away some of the dead wood and introduced a new character; a girlfriend for Stewart. The character was little more than a sounding-board for Stewart's frustrations, but it helped give the story balance.

Stewart was delighted with the rewrite. He told Hitch: 'This is it. You've licked it. Now we can go with it.'

Even then Hitchcock's troubles weren't over. Kim Novak was apprehensive about the picture and uncertain of her talents as an actress. Anxious to postpone the film for as long as possible she claimed her contractual right for a long summer holiday. Columbia agreed. Novak informed Hitchcock that she could not possibly start work until the autumn. By the time the picture did start shooting, Hitchcock was the first to note that Vera Miles had had her baby and could have played the part after all!

Like Doris Day, Novak had her initial problems with Hitchcock, but she turned in a thoroughly credible performance. Sam Taylor felt she was exactly right for the role: 'If he had had a brilliant actress who really created two distinctly different people it would not have been as good. She seemed so naive in the part and that was good. She was always believable. There was no art about it and that's why it worked so well.'

Of the three films Stewart made with Hitchcock in the fifties *Vertigo* was the only one that lost money. Audiences found it a difficult film to watch. They felt baffled and uneasy. Things seemed to go on for too long. This was not the Hitchcock – or the Stewart – they had come to expect.

Another problem was that the film was fatalistic. It was a film about despair. There was no happy ending. The final image as Stewart stands on the bell tower, hands outstretched, having lost for a second time the woman he loves is one of the starkest in all American cinema.

Stewart's performance was arguably the best he had ever given on screen; a brilliantly convincing portrait of a disturbed neurotic unable to overcome the manic obsession that haunts him. It was quite unlike anything he had played previously. So powerful and emotional is his acting that by the time he has reached the point when he attempts to 'recreate' the woman he so desires he is touching greatness.

One of the great errors of the Academy of Motion Picture Arts and Sciences is that it didn't deem Stewart's performance as suitable for nomination in the best actor category. His acting is so convincing that one does not dare contemplate what lies in store for his detective 'Scottie' Ferguson. Almost certainly madness. Possibly suicide. In every way it is a great performance.

With *Vertigo* and his ability to reveal the darkest of dark sides of a character, Stewart came of age – a brilliant actor at the height of his powers. The film was his last for Hitchcock, but there could have been no better or more appropriate way to finish.

15 The Spirit of St Louis

'I've spent two million already. Stewart's
getting ready and there's still no script.'
Jack L. Warner

Jack Warner was just about the only studio head who
failed to profit from Stewart's popularity in the fifties. 'The
most disastrous failure we ever had,' he groaned when it
was all over and he was left to pick up the pieces. Ten
years later he was still sore: 'The picture was a
multi-million dollar turkey. A bomb, a flop, a bust. It never
came close to making a profit.'

The film that created all the havoc was *The Spirit of St
Louis*. It was based on Charles Lindbergh's Pulitzer Prize
winning account of his record 33½-hour solo flight from
New York to Paris in May, 1927. Unfortunately, that was
all it was about. Lindbergh's subsequent, and for many
people more interesting life, which included the tragic
kidnapping and murder of his baby son by Bruno
Hauptmann in 1932 and his years in Europe in the late
thirties when he supposedly held pro-Nazi views were not
included. The film concentrated solely on the flight.

'And that,' said the film's co-writer Wendell Mayes,
'was why no-one went to see it. The picture should have
been called *The Lindbergh Story* or something like that
because when they put it out as *The Spirit of St Louis*
everyone thought it was an old musical. They didn't know
what *The Spirit of St Louis* was. They had no idea it was the
name of a plane.'

Nonetheless, when the project was first mooted it didn't
sound like a bad idea to Jack Warner. Leland Hayward
was the man behind it. He had returned from a successful

ten-year producing stint on Broadway, offering a three picture deal – the stage hit *Mister Roberts, The Spirit of St Louis* and Hemingway's *The Old Man and the Sea*. Henry Fonda and James Cagney would star in the first, Spencer Tracy would appear in the Hemingway picture. The casting of the Lindbergh movie would be decided by mutual consent. Hayward would produce all three pictures.

The deal appealed to Jack Warner who needed all the quality pictures he could get. His studio was not in the best of shape. Like the other Hollywood majors its profits were falling as audiences stayed at home to watch television. Even Doris Day, his major star of the post-war years was beginning to fade. James Dean's star had flickered brightly but briefly. Only the westerns and actioners of John Wayne were regular money-spinners. Hayward's offer was accepted.

At first it seemed as though the deal would be just the shot in the arm the studio needed. *Mister Roberts*, the story of life on an old cargo vessel in the Pacific in the Second World War, went before the cameras first. It grossed $8 million making it one of the most successful movies of the year. With the war movie *Battle Cry* and John Wayne's *The Sea Chase* also among the year's big moneymakers, Warner had every reason for satisfaction. His was the only Hollywood studio with three pictures in the top ten. 1955 belonged to Warner Brothers.

Then came the first hiccup. No one knew who to cast as Lindbergh in *The Spirit of St Louis*. With *Mister Roberts* it had been easy. Fonda had played the role on stage for several years and was the obvious choice, but casting Lindbergh was a very different matter. The only man to come up with a logical choice was director Billy Wilder. He suggested the 25-year-old John Kerr who had just enjoyed a big success on Broadway in *Tea and Sympathy*. Kerr was the right age, but he baulked at playing a man with extreme right-wing political beliefs. He declined and it was back to square one.

Hayward was the next to venture a name. During a meeting with Wilder in Warner's office he mentioned that James Stewart was interested in the role. Stewart was between pictures for Hitchcock, he said. He'd finished with Anthony Mann and what's more Lindbergh had been his boyhood hero. He'd stayed up all night to follow his famous flight and he would be happy to … Hayward got no further. Warner nearly fell out of his chair. 'Are you crazy. He's forty-seven. The guy in our movie is only twenty-five. Forget it!'

Hayward persisted: 'Jack, he's the top star in the country. And you need a big star for this one. It's one man in a plane for two hours for Chrissake. At least think about it.'

'Yeah, I need a star but not one that's pushing fifty,' growled Warner. He glanced at Wilder for support. Wilder shrugged. Stewart would be good for the picture, but he had to agree with Warner.

'This picture's going to cost me millions Leland,' continued Warner. 'You want me to be a laughing stock as well.'

'OK, then what do I tell him,' said Hayward resignedly.

Warner grinned mischievously. 'Tell him anything. Tell him we're looking for a younger man. Tell him he's not right for the part because he's too fat.'

Whether Warner expected Hayward to actually pass on this ludicrous message is unlikely but in the absence of anything else to say and feeling decidedly awkward at having to turn down his friend, Hayward did precisely that. Not surprisingly, Stewart was flabbergasted.

I couldn't believe what I was hearing, but I wanted the part so badly I dieted. I'd never dieted before in my life. I started off at 170lbs and in the end I was so thin I didn't even look like myself. In fact I looked terribly ill. My face was gaunt and I had black rings under my eyes.[1]

As the pounds came off so the calls to Hayward increased. Stewart kept badgering. 'They signed anyone yet?'

'No.'

'Try again. Tell 'em I'll dye my hair. I'm in the cockpit for most of the movie. I'll be wearing a helmet. We'll get by. Try again.'

By now, even the usually assured and confident Hayward was becoming worried by the situation. Pre-production work was well under way and three replicas of Lindbergh's single-engine Ryan were already ready and waiting. Wilder was toiling away on the script and Jack Warner was becoming impatient. The budget was rising by the day. His original investment of one million dollars for the rights to film Lindbergh's book was looking decidedly precarious.

Hayward once again tackled Warner. And this time the studio boss gave way. Too much money had already been spent. He now had no choice but to go with a major star. He agreed on Stewart and consoled himself with the thought that if *The Spirit of St Louis* became a Jimmy Stewart picture, the film would at least make a profit or at the very worst break even. He relaxed.

Then came more bad news. Wilder had only completed some forty pages of script. This time Warner nearly had convulsions. 'What the hell has he been doing?' he cried. 'Get 'em up here. I want to see the script. Get 'em all up here – Wilder, Hayward, Mayes. And anyone else who's costing me money.'

Wilder heard of the summons. He was an Oscar winner several times over. He was not a man given to obeying commands from Hollywood moguls. He refused. He sent a message to Warner's office. He never showed one of his scripts to anyone, not even a studio head, until it was finished.

Warner called him on the phone. 'But Billy', he wailed, changing from tyrannical studio head to hard-done-by producer within seconds. 'I've spent two million already. Stewart's getting ready and there's still no script. Be reasonable.' Wilder said he would make a halfway gesture. He wouldn't let Warner read the script but he would come to his office and explain in detail how things were working out. Warner accepted that this was better than nothing and agreed. He'd expected just Wilder. Instead, he got Mayes and Hayward as well. Even for a man who'd stood eyeball to eyeball with such rebellious stars as Errol Flynn and Bette Davis the scene that unfolded before him that afternoon was a new experience.

Wilder's co-writer Wendell Mayes narrated the story. Leland Hayward (who fancied himself as being musical) hummed the still unwritten score and Wilder filled in with all the necessary plane noises such as the starting of the engine and the whirring of the propellor.

The spectacle of three grown men indulging in such a pantomime softened Warner's attitude. The other Warner executives at the meeting complained that they were being conned. Warner knew it too but for the first time since active work had started on *The Spirit of St Louis* he'd actually enjoyed himself. He also knew when he was beaten. 'OK boys, great stuff. Just bring me in a great picture.'

All of which was easier said than done. Wilder might have exuded confidence during the show in Warner's office, but secretly he was more than a little worried about his work on the picture. His main problem was that he was in uncharted waters. More a comedy man and at home with stars of the calibre of Marilyn Monroe and Audrey Hepburn he found himself in something of a straitjacket. Normally, if he ran into a problem, he could write himself out of it, adding scenes, changing existing ones, reworking a plotline. On *The Spirit of St Louis* he was trapped. His film depicted one man's solo flight from one country to another. Seventy-five per cent of the action took place in the cockpit of the plane. He had 135 minutes of screentime to fill.

The most annoying thing about the situation was that he had no one to blame but himself. He had wanted to make the picture. He had signed for it because, like Stewart, he regarded Lindbergh as something of a heroic figure. He too had marvelled at his exploits when he was a young reporter in Berlin in the late twenties. Unfortunately, recreating those heady days proved much more difficult than he had imagined.

His biggest problem was that he could not go forward in time. The film ended with Lindbergh landing in Paris. All he could do therefore was to flashback and as often as possible to Lindbergh's early days as an airmail pilot and as a young barnstormer in the rural Mid West. He even included a fictional knockabout episode in which

Lindbergh teaches a plucky priest to fly so that he can be nearer to God.

Most audacious of all was his introduction of a fly for Stewart to talk to during the flight. As there was no radio in the original plane Lindbergh had no one to talk to but himself. The introduction of the fly, who hops aboard on Stewart's packet of sandwiches, allowed the pilot to indulge in whimsical conversations with the insect. It was a crazy piece of invention, but it worked. When a journalist later asked if Stewart had expressed any doubts about talking to an insect, Wilder replied: 'Of course not. He's used to it. He's been talking to agents and studio heads all his life.'

Stewart revelled in recreating his boyhood hero on film. He studied old newsreel footage of the planes of the time and of Lindbergh's landing in Paris. He observed Lindbergh's mannerisms and the way he walked and talked. He even managed to participate in the occasional flying sequence although he did admit to disappointment when Warner refused to allow him to actually land the plane for the waiting crowds at Le Bourqet, Paris at the climax to the momentous flight. Another pilot brought the plane down; Stewart was allowed the close-ups in the taxiing shots.

Wilder and Stewart got along well together during shooting, enjoying long conversations about the character and achievements of their mutual hero. Stewart even went so far as to dare Wilder to wing walk for ten minutes before shooting began, just to prove that Wilder's heart was in the right place. Wilder accepted the wager and won.

For Wilder though, all the camaraderie counted for nothing. The film continued to be a nightmare. He moaned:

We had to cover such a vast area because all the locations had to be exactly right. We had to fly the actual replica of the plane and we had unbelievable mechanical problems. We could not communicate with the plane when it was up in the sky so it had to land, get the instructions and then take off again. We had other planes in the air to film the planes we were shooting. If there were too many holdups your day was gone. Then the weather didn't match. It really needed a director like John Frankenheimer, a man with enormous patience for technical details. I'm not an outdoor man. I've never done a western. I think I should confine myself to bedrooms, maybe.[2]

Lindbergh turned up only once during shooting, when the company began filming at the Long Island location. He stayed just long enough to say a brief 'hello' to the cast and to check out the accuracy of Paul Mantz's full-scale model of his original plane. The model had been lovingly recreated by Mantz from original blueprints and was much admired by Lindbergh.

His views on the finished film, however, were more muted. In fact, the only moment that seemed to impress him was when Stewart, about to start the engine, tapped the oil gauge. Being a pilot himself Stewart had done this automatically. 'When you were flying a reciprocating engine that was a natural thing to do. The oil-pressure gauge is of vital importance when the engine is turning over, because if the oil-pressure gauge isn't rising, it means the pistons aren't getting lubricated.'

The opportunity to socialize with Lindbergh during the filming was equally brief. Remembered Stewart:

He was a very quiet man. He didn't say much when he visited the set in New York and we didn't really have much chance to get to know him when he gave us a call in Hollywood.

He called Gloria and I at home one evening about five. He said 'I'm out at the airport and I was wondering what you were doing for dinner.' I told him that we were going to Chasen's and he said: 'I'll be there in twenty-five minutes.'

We took him to Chasen's. He was very pleasant. I think we were just beginning to get to know him when poor Dave Chasen came up and said: 'Mr Lindbergh, I have a terrible thing to tell you and I apologize, believe me. I made a point of not saying anything to anyone and keeping your visit quiet, but there are forty people outside, newspaper people with cameras.'

Lindbergh said: 'Do you have a back door out of the kitchen? I'll use that. Would you get me a taxi.' He said goodbye, thanked us and left through the back way. And that's the last we saw of him.[3]

Wilder's insistence that *The Spirit of St Louis* be as accurate as possible meant that he shot at key points along the actual route of Lindbergh's journey. Filming took place in New York, Nova Scotia, Newfoundland, the Irish Coast, across the Channel and in Paris. The extensive location work tipped the budget from $5 million to $6 million. Originally, it had been set at $2 million.

When he viewed the finished film at his private theatre at Burbank, Jack L. Warner knew that he was doomed. There was simply nothing on screen that would make interesting entertainment for an audience used to the everyday convenience of jet travel. The 135 minutes seemed as long if not longer than Lindbergh's original flight.

He couldn't blame Wilder who, under the circumstances, had turned in a respectable and occasionally inspiring picture. He couldn't blame Stewart. His was a many layered, thoughtful performance, full of texture and insight. Despite his age and unconvincing reddish hair he had made Lindbergh a very real person.

Technically, the film was superb, but as the closing credits rolled and the lights went up in the viewing theatre everyone there knew that the film didn't stand a chance of making its money back. The spirit of James Dean was still alive in the movie houses, and there was a new hero alive and well on the big screen – Elvis Presley plus Rock 'n' Roll. The story of the epic journey of a rickety old plane across the Atlantic was hardly going to satisfy the teenagers.

In the viewing theatre there was an awkward silence. 'Great music score,' said Warner to composer Franz Waxman. Waxman nodded appreciatively. The cameramen came in for similar praise.

Wilder remained silent. 'Good script Billy ...' began Warner.

Wilder held up his hand. 'You don't have to say it Jack.

It doesn't work. We all know that.' He tried manfully to conjure up some optimism. 'But who knows. Audiences are fickle. There are surprises all the time.'

'Not this big,' muttered Warner gloomily. 'The only damned air movies that ever made money were war movies, *Wings*, *The Dawn Patrol*, stuff like that.'

Leland Hayward was as disappointed as anyone with the final result, but he kept his own counsel. He knew it would take all the expertise of the Warner publicity men to get the film to break even let alone make a profit.

In the end they didn't make it. The general rule of thumb in Hollywood is that a film needs to take two and a half times its production cost to get into the black which would have meant a 'take' somewhere in the region of $15 million. By the end of 1957 *The Spirit of St Louis* had grossed only $2.6 million and was tailing off fast. In Lindbergh's home town it took barely enough money to pay the staff of the cinema at which it was showing. By 1958 the accountants stopped counting, probably because they couldn't find anything left to count. 'A disastrous failure,' said Warner. 'Every studio has them from time to time, but this was one of the worst. We should never have put it into production.'

A year later, Warners showed a deficit of a million dollars. It was the first time in twenty years that the studio had been in the red. Much of its perilous financial position was put down to the failure of *The Spirit of St Louis* and also the other Leland Hayward fiasco that followed it, *The Old Man and the Sea*. There was no talking to a fly this time. Instead, Spencer Tracy, as Hemingway's famous Cuban fisherman, spent eighty-five minutes talking to himself. Those audiences who bothered to turn up drifted quickly into a deep sleep.

Just about the only person who had any real reason for satisfaction was Stewart. His playing was likeably sharp and pointed. In his book Lindbergh had come over as a quietly tenacious young pioneer imbued with a kind of idealistic innocence. Stewart caught much of his hero's idealism and strength of will and although a little uncertain in the flashbacks was superb when stressing the flier's sense of isolation and his increasing fatigue and boredom. One scene, when he falls asleep at the controls and is awakened from his dive by a shaft of sunlight filtering through the cockpit, is an especially fine piece of screencraft. So too was his recreation of Lindbergh's famous yell: 'Which way to Ireland?' as his plane swoops low across the coast and above some startled fishermen. Such scenes, though, were few and far between. For most audiences it was a long haul.

It was left to Billy Wilder to sum it all up: 'A bad decision', he said. 'I succeeded with a couple of moments but I missed creating the character.' Then, as an afterthought, he quipped: 'I felt sorry for Jack Warner. I thought of offering him his money back but then I thought he might take it.'

Footnotes

1. *Everybody's Man*, Jhan Robbins, Robson Books (1985)
2. *Billy Wilder in Hollywood*, Maurice Zolotow, W.H. Allen (1977)
3. *Film Comment* (March–April 1990)

16   Otto and a Murder

'James Stewart, the star, came and stood
by the camera and performed for me
alone. It was a lesson I've never
forgotten.'

George C. Scott

The main problem facing Stewart as the fifties drew to a
close was one that presented itself to many Hollywood
stars of his generation: how to stop being a romantic lead
and accept that, at 51, he was now past the age of wooing
such stars as Kim Novak, Grace Kelly and Doris Day.

The new situation was by no means an easy one to come
to terms with. Apart from the occasional film (*The Greatest
Show on Earth, The Spirit of St Louis*) Stewart had invariably
been involved romantically on screen. Audiences
expected it of their leading stars and studios duly
provided it, and for a time people like Gary Cooper, Clark
Gable, Fred Astaire, and Stewart managed to get away
with it. A piece of astute makeup, some subtle lighting and
a slight thickening or dyeing of the hair invariably
managed to create the illusion that they were somewhat
younger than they actually were.

In the end, however, the spectacle of a middle-aged
man romancing a woman half his age tended to become a
little ludicrous if not downright embarrassing. After he
had played opposite Kim Novak once more in Columbia's
Bell, Book and Candle, a slight but charming comedy about
witchcraft in contemporary New York, Stewart was forced
to forego the romantic side of things and concentrate on
roles that cast him as either a bachelor or a happily
married man with a family. The abrupt change of pace cut
his role opportunities at a stroke.

Reassurance came from an unlikely quarter, the controversial film-maker Otto Preminger who suggested that there might be life after screen romance when he offered Stewart a role that many Hollywood actors had had their eyes on for some time – that of the small-town lawyer Paul Biegler in *Anatomy of a Murder*.

The film was based on the then hot bestseller by Robert Traver who based his seamy tale on a case he himself had actually defended in Marquette, Michigan in 1952. The case centred on a US army lieutenant who shot and killed a local bar proprietor who had supposedly raped his wife. The trial turned on two main questions. Was the wife of the lieutenant telling the truth when she stated she had been raped and was the lieutenant 'temporarily insane' when he committed the crime?

Stewart's role was, on the face of it, perfect casting – a warm, folksy, slightly absent-minded man with a love of jazz and fishing and who has more or less accepted the fact that he will never amount to anything but a small-town lawyer. Beneath the surface, however, he is a man harbouring resentments, mainly because he has been passed over for the job of public prosecutor. When the case is offered he accepts it eagerly. As he prepares his defence he reveals something of a cunning and cynical nature. He even harbours doubts about the innocence and morality of his client. In court, he pulls out all the stops, making dramatic interventions and bringing a last-minute witness to the stand.

The film was perfect Preminger material. During the fifties he had made a name, and large profits, for himself with a series of controversial films that often flew in the face of the censorship of the time and went into release without the so-called essential Motion Picture Code Seal of Approval.

The sex comedy *The Moon is Blue* had been one such Preminger excursion. *The Man with the Golden Arm*, a harrowing tale of drug addiction, had been another. *Anatomy of a Murder*, which pulled no punches in its clinical and outspoken handling of the subject of rape, was the perfect follow-up. The script included words such as 'intercourse', 'contraceptive', 'spermatogenesis' and 'sexual climax'. It also included direct references to women's panties. It asked the question 'Can you prove rape?' and then went to exceptional lengths and immense clinical detail to prove that you could.

Wendell Mayes' script was the most demanding to have come Stewart's way since *It's a Wonderful Life*. Full of long, impassioned courtroom sequences it demanded intense concentration. When he and Gloria took off for a safari to India Stewart took the script along with him for extra company. Many nights, Gloria would be sound asleep in their tent while Stewart read long into the early hours preparing for what was to become one of his most celebrated portrayals. Stewart said:

> It was worth all the extra effort. I spent a lot of time memorizing my lines for that movie. The picture demanded an awful lot of time and thought. As the defence attorney I knew I had to be glibber than usual. Trial lawyers are neither shy nor inarticulate. I read my script each night until I fell asleep. When I got back to the States I felt better prepared physically and mentally than I'd ever been.[1]

The only thing that slightly bothered him was the thought of working with the terrible Otto who had gained notoriety for being something of an ogre on set. Jean Seberg had been unmercifully bullied when filming *Saint Joan*, David Niven hadn't enjoyed *Bonjour Tristesse* one little bit and Darryl F. Zanuck was constantly at loggerheads with the film-maker when he had him under contract at 20th Century Fox in the forties.

Later, Faye Dunaway made headlines when she refused to be signed to a personal contract and Robert Mitchum was actually sacked after just three days work on the thriller *Rosebud*. Said the unrepentant Mitchum:

> I reported at six o'clock in the morning and just for the fun of it, imitated his German accent and mannerisms for the crew. Old Otto came up to me screaming: 'You've been drinking.' I told him that I did my share of drinking but not at 6 a.m. for God's Sake. But he kept yelling. I tried to break the tension on the set by imitating him again and he almost

140

had a stroke. He flew into a rage. 'You're through ... fired.'

I wasn't mad. Hell, I thought Otto was funny. I don't believe he really wanted to fire me. He just lost his temper and it was too late. I didn't care one way or the other. It's funny, Preminger objected to drinking actors, but he replaced me with Peter O'Toole. Hell, that's like replacing Ray Charles with Helen Keller.[2]

For a while it seemed as though it might also be something of a rough ride on *Anatomy of a Murder*. A blazing row ensued before a single camera turned. Stewart was not aware of it at the time. He was still in India on safari. When he left for India his former co-star at MGM, Lana Turner, had been signed to play the lieutenant's wife. On his return Turner had vanished from the scene and been replaced by the younger Lee Remick who had just made a breakthrough in Kazan's *A Face in the Crowd*. The reason, he was told, had nothing to do with Turner's dissatisfaction with her role. It had to do with her wardrobe.

The *New York Daily News* was quick to pounce on the Preminger/Turner row. Otto had always been good copy and so too had Turner. Just a year earlier, 1958, she had been the participant in a real-life court trial when her 14-year-old daughter fatally stabbed the actress's then lover Johnny Stompanato. When she and Otto locked horns the paper was quick with the headlines: 'Lana Gives Up Juicy Role in Film Rhubarb'. Other papers also reported the incident in full.

Both Preminger and Turner came up with different accounts of what had happened. Preminger's version was that he and his costume co-ordinator selected a pair of slacks in a Beverly Hills shop and asked Turner to meet them there for a fitting. Miss Turner failed to appear.

Preminger then received a call from Turner's agent who insisted that his client's wardrobe should, as usual, be designed by the fashionable Jean-Louis. Preminger pointed out that Turner's role was that of the wife of a second lieutenant who would hardly walk around in clothes made by a top Hollywood designer. She won't do it, came the reply. 'OK,' snapped Preminger, 'send me a letter stating she would like to cancel her contract and I'll find someone else.'

The letter duly arrived and Preminger offered the role to Lee Remick. 'They thought I was bluffing,' said Otto defiantly, 'but no one decides what to wear in my films but me.'

Lana Turner had a different story to tell. She said:

I have never favoured ready-to-wear clothing on screen. So I suggested that my dressmaker run up the kind of suit she had in mind.

The next evening I answered the telephone and heard a male voice with a thick Viennese accent, shouting at me.

'You *bitch*! This is Otto Preminger,' he yelled. 'You are to understand that this is *my* production. You think you are the great star? *You* will make the decisions. No!' Then, after more expletives, he screamed: '*I* vill choose your clothes you ...'

I banged down the receiver then immediately telephoned my agent: 'Get me out of *Anatomy of a Murder*. I can't possibly work with that man.[3]

And so saying, she went. The mutterings among the cast which also included Ben Gazzara, Arthur O'Connell and Eve Arden, were that if this kind of thing could happen over a pair of slacks what else was in store when shooting actually started. Not much, as it turned out. Otto seemed to have rid himself of all his fury before a camera turned. During filming he was sweetness itself. He said: 'People don't really understand me. I only get angry at one thing and that is when people don't try. Then I get annoyed. All of the actors who have worked with me will work with me again – just ask them.'

Preminger set himself the task of completing *Anatomy of a Murder* in just eight weeks. It was a tight schedule for such a large picture, especially as all of it was to be photographed on actual locations in the remote windswept town of Marquette, some 400 miles north of Detroit. 'I am an impatient man,' he said. 'I never shoot more than is absolutely necessary. I don't shoot long.'

He was so confident that he could stay on schedule that he booked the film into three major theatres, one in New

York, the others in Chicago and Los Angeles, before he began filming. He said:

> We started on March 23 in Michigan and we finished in eight weeks. The last shooting day was May 16. A month later I previewed the picture in San Francisco. It was an obvious success with the public. I didn't change or cut anything and it went right into release. The book had just gone into paperback so we were lucky in that respect. The film grossed more than two million in six weeks.[4]

Stewart's work was so concentrated that he had just one afternoon off during the entire eight-week shoot. Even then he made certain that he took time out to help the then up and coming actor George C. Scott who had been cast as his adversary in the film – a sharp-tongued big-city prosecutor. Scott had made only one previous film and was still something of a green actor as far as movies were concerned.

When he was required to play a long and highly demanding scene in the movie, Stewart told him that he would read for him off-camera. Often, the actor playing opposite will take a rest. His face is not needed, nor his voice. Someone else will read lines to get the right reaction.

The most famous occasion when this occurred was during the filming of *On the Waterfront* when Marlon Brando and Rod Steiger played the taxi scene, one of the most celebrated in the history of American movies. Brando, having completed his scenes, had left at four o'clock leaving the film's director Elia Kazan, to feed the appropriate lines to Steiger. Thanks to Stewart no such occasion arose during the filming of *Anatomy of a Murder*. Scott said:

> I was very anxious about things. Jim was very kind in rehearsing. We had long courtroom scenes. And lots and lots of words but I knew his reputation and I had expected him to be kind in that regard.
>
> But what I didn't expect and what stunned me was what happened after we'd finished the coverage on Jim and the camera turned around on me. Some actors have a

tendency to kind of sidle up to the camera (you know, they're off camera) and sort of phone it in from there. But not Mr Stewart. The sleeves came down. The cuffs were closed. The tie went up. The collar was closed. The vest was buttoned. The suit jacket went on and James Stewart, the star, came and stood by the camera and performed for me alone. It was a lesson I've never forgotten.[5]

Preminger was another who had every reason to admire Stewart's professionalism.

One of the most professional of actors, a joy to work with, a man who exerts a very healthy influence on the whole cast. He is not only a brilliant actor but a rare man on a personal level as well. We only worked together the once but I still feel close to him. It's as though we had finished working on the film yesterday.[6]

Many critics rated Stewart's Paul Biegler as one of the best characterizations of his career. In *The New York Times* Bosley Crowther wrote that the film was as good a courtroom drama as he had ever seen and praised Stewart for the manner in which he revealed the character of Biegler: 'Slowly and subtly he presents us with a warm, clever, adroit and complex man and, most particularly, a portrait of a trial lawyer in action which will be difficult for anyone to surpass.'

Campbell Dixon in London's *Daily Telegraph* said: 'James Stewart makes the Clarence Darrow of the piece the embodiment of shrewdness and homespun charm.'

The entire cast came in for praise from *Saturday Review:* ... the marvellously equivocal portraits provided in *Anatomy of a Murder* by James Stewart, Lee Remick, Ben Gazzara and George Scott reveal complexities in character such as rarely are seen on the American screen.'

Such was the universal praise for his performance that the jury at the Venice Film Festival named Stewart best actor of the festival in September 1959. All of which turned Stewart's mind once more in the direction of Oscars. Never one to be carried away by too much over confidence he genuinely thought he had a chance, especially when The New York Critics voted him best actor ahead of Charlton Heston for *Ben-Hur*.

Despite the fact that *Anatomy of a Murder* failed to figure in any of The Golden Globe awards (for many a bad portent), Stewart still had sufficient faith in himself and the picture when the nominations were announced. Preminger (who never won an Academy Award) missed out as best director, but the film did pick up a healthy seven nominations including nods for best picture, best screenplay, cinematography and editing. George C. Scott and Arthur O'Connell (as Stewart's boozy old colleague) were both named in the supporting actor category and Stewart landed his expected mention for best actor.

Ben-Hur was the obvious favourite with twelve nominations, but 1959 was a good year and with such strong contenders as *Some Like it Hot*, *The Nun's Story* and *The Diary of Anne Frank*, there was every chance that Ben-Hur's chariot could be halted.

Gloria Stewart remembered the evening rather more vividly than Stewart himself. She said:

> One of the protective devices the nominees use to soften the pangs of suspense is to crouch down in their seats muttering to themselves: 'I can't win, I won't win'. But Jimmy was quite honest with himself. He surprised me. He sat there saying: 'I might just win. I can't help thinking I've got a good chance.'
>
> I had my hand on his arm and it was like keeping in touch with a tuning fork. Thank heaven it was over quickly. As soon as Hugh Griffith won the supporting actor award for his role as the sheik in *Ben-Hur* Jim and I knew it would be a clean sweep; so when Charlton Heston won for best actor it wasn't much of a shock. By that time *Ben-Hur* had swept the board. I don't mean that Jim wasn't disappointed but I was more emotionally rocked than he was.[7]

Even though it didn't register a single Oscar win *Anatomy of a Murder* remains one of Stewart's finest achievements. Unlike so many pictures it doesn't date. Its freshness combined with its controversial content make it seem as modern as many of the movies of the eighties and

In Hitchcock's *The Man Who Knew Too Much* (1956) things look bad in a London taxidermist's, but it's only a Hitchcock red herring!

This time things seem much more serious as Stewart learns of an assassination plot from a dying agent in *The Man Who Knew Too Much* (1956)

Stewart in the opening
sequence from Hitchcock's
masterpiece *Vertigo* (1958)

The beginning of a fatal obsession. Stewart and Kim Novak in
Vertigo (1958)

Off set during the making of *Anatomy of a Murder* (1959).
Examining vital evidence with Ben Gazzara and
Otto Preminger

Stewart in *Anatomy of a Murder* (1959) defending his client
Ben Gazzara

Throwing himself on the mercy of the court. George C. Scott
looks on in disbelief. Another scene from Preminger's
Anatomy of a Murder (1959)

Stewart in one of his most celebrated roles of the sixties as the
Virginia farmer who becomes caught up in the Civil War in
Shenandoah (1965)

Stranded in the desert with Richard Attenborough and a planeload of male passengers in *Flight of the Phoenix* (1965)

Stewart battling against the elements in his search for a missing Hereford bull in *The Rare Breed* (1966)

nineties. None of the issues in the story is clear cut. People are shown with unsentimental honesty and to be complex and contradictory. There are no neat ends; the film is full of small, cleverly integrated scenes with Stewart, balanced against the rest of the film, serving a dramatic purpose.

As the man who is 'too pure for the impurities of the law' he provides the one secure anchor for audience sympathies. Today, some thirty years on, his Paul Biegler remains one of the great screen lawyers.

Yet for all this he took a chance with the part. There were many who felt that he should not have lent his name to the picture. This was not the Jimmy Stewart they expected or wanted to see. Said Stewart:

You know I got an awful lot of letters after *Anatomy of a Murder*. You let us down, they said. I'm not going to your pictures anymore. I take my family to see a Jimmy Stewart picture and you're up there in court talking dirty and holding up women's panties. But I didn't think *Anatomy of a Murder* was in bad taste or offensive. And if anything like it came along again I'd just have to take it ... parts like that don't come along every day.

As for working with the terrible Otto?

No trouble. I'd work with him again tomorrow if he asked me. A first rate film-maker. I think it was Darryl Zanuck who said 'Otto is a very good and very talented director. But he makes either great or crazy pictures. Nothing in between. I think our *Anatomy of a Murder* was one of the great ones.'

Footnotes

1. *Saturday Evening Post* (March 1961)
2. *Robert Mitchum on the Screen*, Alvin H. Marrill, Barnes (1978)
3. *Lana*, New English Library (1982)
4. *Films & Filming*, (November 1959)
5. *Lincoln Center Tribute to James Stewart* (April 1990)
6. *Preminger, An Autobiography*, Doubleday (1977)
7. *Saturday Evening Post* (February 1961)

17   John Ford's Two-and-a-half

'People just liked him. He played himself
but he played the character.'

John Ford

In the early sixties Stewart sought and found solace with
his family. From August 1959 to late in 1960 he took his
first break from the cameras since the war, travelling with
Gloria and, when vacations allowed, his children, to many
different parts of the world.

Since their marriage James and Gloria had become
inveterate travellers journeying sometimes with friends to
Scotland, Spain, India and South America where in Chile,
Argentina and Peru they found tranquillity fishing and
studying wildlife.

Stewart badly needed the break. Professionally, it had
been a disappointing time. The two pictures he had made
following *Anatomy* had failed to capitalize on the success
of the Preminger movie. *The FBI Story* was a routine
history of the bureau seen through the eyes of a pioneer
agent and *The Mountain Road*, a dull, ponderous anti-war
film about an American demolition team operating in
China in the Second World War. Stewart would have
preferred to have played the on-the-run hero of
Hitchcock's *North By Northwest*, a role he had much
coveted but which had always been lined up by Hitch for
his other top star Cary Grant. Stewart found it difficult to
hide his disappointment.

His private life too was marred by sadness as he lost two
of his closest friends. In January 1960, the lovely, mercurial
Margaret Sullavan, aged just forty-nine, took her life after
a long and valiant struggle with deafness, and in May of

the following year Gary Cooper succumbed to cancer. Just a month earlier Stewart had accepted a special Oscar awarded to Cooper for his 'many memorable screen performances and the international recognition he had gained for the motion picture industry'.

Cooper had been too ill to attend. An emotional Stewart, handed the award by William Wyler, gulped back his tears and said softly: 'We're all very proud of you Coop. All of us are very proud.' Unable to continue he left the stage.

Work, when it did come again, arrived in the form of a western – *Two Rode Together*. On the face of it a western seemed this time to be something of a retrograde step. Stewart was now fifty-four, too old perhaps to be back in the saddle. There was, however, a bonus. The movie was to be directed by John Ford. Stewart had been lucky in that he had worked with most of the top film-makers in Hollywood. Ford, though, had always escaped him. Duke Wayne had been a Ford regular with *Stagecoach, She Wore a Yellow Ribbon* and others; so too had Hank Fonda who had starred in *Young Mr Lincoln, The Grapes Of Wrath* and *My Darling Clementine*. Now, at last, it was Stewart's turn.

The film focused on two men, one a cynical Texas lawman (Stewart), the other an idealistic army lieutenant (Richard Widmark) who set out to rescue some white captives being held by the Comanches.

For Ford it was a case of déjà vu. He had already filmed a similar story some five years earlier when he'd made *The Searchers*. But for Stewart the film offered the chance to play a character well out of the Jimmy Stewart mould, a mean-spirited mercenary whose actions are entirely motivated by money. His sheriff, when faced with the decision of going after the Indians, asks not 'Can we save the captives?' but 'What's in it for me?' When he is assured that he will receive $500 for every white he brings back he agrees to the mission.

As a story it didn't amount to much and at first Ford had turned it down. 'A piece of junk,' he snarled when the Columbia executives presented him with the screenplay. As a favour, pleaded the studio. Only if you let me rewrite the script, said Ford. Agreed!

Ford's veteran collaborator Frank Nugent was brought

in. Ford still didn't like it. He grumbled. 'It's still crap.' By then, however, he was committed.

Stewart had been warned about Ford. Everyone, it seemed, had their favourite horror stories about the director. Frank Capra called: 'Watch out for him Jimmy – he's half saint, halt satan; half possible, half impossible, half genius, and half Irish.' He laughed. 'Things will be tough, but good luck anyway.'

Duke Wayne, Maureen O'Hara, Spencer Tracy and others also offered advice on how to best deal with the coming ordeal. Hank Fonda came up with the most ominous warning. Ford, he said, could be mean. Worse, he could be violent. He recalled the filming of *Mister Roberts*.

A few days after shooting had begun he had become anxious about the amount of broad Irish humour Ford was injecting into the film – it seemed misplaced. He went to see Ford in his office. He knew him well by then but he quickly learned that the past counted for nothing.

'You don't like the way I'm directing this movie?' snapped Ford from behind his desk, glaring fiercely at Fonda with his non-patched eye.

'Well, no Pappy. Most of it's OK. It's just that I know this play. I was in it a long time on Broadway and although there is humour in it it's essentially a serious piece of work. It's about ...'

'I *know* what it's about,' roared Ford, '... and it isn't a play anymore, it's a movie. And it's *my* movie.' And with that he got up, walked around his desk and struck Fonda a firm blow on the jaw. He packed quite a punch and Fonda went sprawling. More puzzled than hurt, Fonda tried to figure out what to do next. He could hardly hit back. Ford was a much older man. So he did nothing. Without uttering another word he shook his head, clambered to his feet and left.

Fifteen minutes later Ford sought him out and apologized. Fonda would have none of it. The film was the first he and Ford had made together for almost ten years. It was meant to have been a dream reunion. Instead, it marked the beginning of a long and bitter feud.

A morose Ford went on a bender and drank himself into oblivion. The producer – the luckless Leland Hayward –

closed the picture for five days. When they eventually returned from the Honolulu locations to Hollywood an alcoholic Ford went down with a ruptured gall bladder. Mervyn LeRoy took over. Fonda and Ford didn't speak to each other for years.

They still weren't talking when Stewart reported for the first day's shooting on *Two Rode Together*. Stewart's most immediate problem was how he should address the master film-maker. Wayne, he knew, called him 'Coach'. Fonda preferred 'Pappy'. There were other names too including 'Admiral', 'Skipper' and 'The Old Man'. Also used quite frequently although never to his face, was 'That Old Sonofabitch'. Stewart settled on 'Boss'. It seemed the safest and most respectful form of address.

That Ford was not at all interested in *Two Rode Together* became immediately apparent to all those connected with the picture. Crotchety and bad-tempered, he would chew at the corner of his handkerchief or puff at a cigar and engage in sarcastic taunts whenever things didn't go quite to plan. He also didn't give a damn how he looked. His shirt collars were invariably frayed, the seats of his pants shiny. His socks rarely matched. Sometimes he would show up with an old necktie wrapped around his waist for a belt.

His temper wasn't improved by the fact that many of the cronies he liked to mix with off set weren't connected with the picture. There was no Wayne, no Maureen O'Hara, no Ben Johnson. Ward Bond and Victor McLaglen had recently passed away and even his favourite cameramen, Bill Clothier and Bert Glennon weren't on hand.

Stewart found his direction bewildering.

In a Ford film you were never exactly sure of what was going to happen next. And that's the way he wanted it. His crew knew exactly what was going to happen. His assistants knew exactly what was going to happen. The only people who didn't seem to know were the actors.

His direction took the form of asides. Sometimes he'd put his hand across his mouth so that others couldn't hear what he was saying to you. On *Two Rode Together* he told me to watch out for Dick Widmark because he was a good actor and that he would start scene stealing if I didn't watch him. Later, I learned he'd told Dick the same thing about me. He liked things to be tense. He liked actors to be suspicious of other actors.

On occasion he also revealed a sadistic streak. For a long dialogue scene between Stewart and Widmark, one in which they talk whilst sitting on a log in front of a river, he had the cameraman and crew wade into the river early on a freezing cold morning and photograph the entire scene from the water. The scene would have been just as effective from any other angle, but Ford insisted. He was not a popular man that day. Stars and crew were close to open rebellion.

The critical reaction to *Two Rode Together* was poor, and the public didn't much care for it either. Its box-office gross was $1.5 million in a year when hit movies were taking anything between $3 and $12 million. Ford disowned it. 'It was still a load of crap. I didn't enjoy the damn thing. I just tried to make Stewart's character as humorous as possible.'

He was much more positive about things a year later when he called on Stewart again, this time to co-star with John Wayne in *The Man Who Shot Liberty Valance*.

It was a picture close to Ford's heart, the story of an idealistic young lawyer who arrives in the town of Shinbone determined to set up a law practice and bring civilization to the West. Because he is believed to have gunned down the notorious outlaw Liberty Valance he rises to become senator of his State. The reputation is undeserved. His close friend, rancher John Wayne, did the actual killing, but he allows the myth to remain because he sees in Stewart qualities that he himself does not possess and that Stewart is the man to take the territory into Statehood. Told in flashback at the time of Wayne's pauper burial, the film was a then innovative commentary on the merging of the Old West with the new.

The realization that things were changing in Hollywood was brought home forcibly during the filming of *The Man Who Shot Liberty Valance*.

Paramount's initial reaction when presented with the script was one of indifference. A year earlier they'd suffered a financial disaster with Marlon Brando's over budget *One-Eyed Jacks*. They were not at all eager to venture West again even if the film was to be directed by the only man ever to have won four Oscars for direction.

That Ford should have trouble setting up a production caused surprise in Hollywood. That he should have trouble setting up a *western* caused amazement. A few years earlier he had experienced no trouble in this regard. Studios had even allowed him to indulge in the occasional small-budget personal production such as *The Sun Shines Bright*. Now it seemed his reputation counted for nothing. It was a sobering and depressing experience and proof that the old Hollywood was rapidly being overtaken by the new.

In the end it was Wayne's name that got the picture off the ground. He had signed a multi-picture deal with Paramount and with Stewart alongside him, the studio agreed to take a chance with the picture. Even then they agreed to finance only half of the $3.2 million production. Ford had to spend some five months raising the other $1.6 million. There was no Technicolor. The studio insisted on black and white. The locations were few. Much of the film was shot in the studio.

The wait disillusioned Ford. Optimistic and eager at first he had been sapped of much of his energy by the time the picture rolled. Heavily dependent on alcohol, he needled his actors even more than usual. It was Wayne who caught the brunt of it. Stewart said:

Ford was tough on that movie. And when I say tough I mean really tough. He used to get to the Duke and I would feel for him.

Some days Duke would say: 'How come the boss don't get on to you?' Well, my turn came all right – just two weeks before we finished the picture. There was a funeral scene with a coffin. Woody Strode, who was a veteran of many Ford films, had been made to look old – plus overalls and a hat.

Ford came over to me and asked what I thought of the costume. I said it was a bit Uncle Remus-like and then

almost immediately wished I'd bitten my tongue. I knew
I'd made a mistake.

'And what's wrong with Uncle Remus?'
'Waal ... nothing boss.'
'Woody, Duke, everybody, come over here. Look at
Woody, look at his costume. One of the *players* seems to
have some objection. One of the *players* here doesn't seem
to like Uncle Remus. As a matter of fact I'm not at all sure
he even likes negroes.'
Ford crashed on. Stewart wished the ground would
open up and swallow him. Most of the crew were grinning
– certainly Wayne was. Later, after the tirade was over he
came across and, in a Ford-like gesture, put his hand in
front of his mouth and whispered: 'Ya thought you were
goin to make it right through didn't ya.'
Stewart's performance in *The Man Who Shot Liberty
Valance* was one of the most impressive he gave in the
sixties. A combination of the idealistic Mr Smith and his
lawyer in *Anatomy of a Murder*, it required him to age from
a youthful man in his late twenties to a mature political
figure. The early scenes were by no means easy for a man
in his mid-fifties but he played them with more conviction
than he had done in *The Spirit of St Louis* and in the later
sequences he was quite superb as a crusader determined
to make The West a place fit for decent people. Wayne had
top billing and his character was the tragic cornerstone of
the film. It was the sincerity and intelligence of Stewart's
acting, however, that held the film together.
And it is to Stewart, in the final moments of the film,
that the newspaper editor who has listened to Stewart's
story, utters one of the immortal lines in movie history.
When Stewart asks him if he is going to reveal that he did
not, after all, kill Liberty Valance, the newspaper man
shakes his head: 'This is the West sir; when the legend
becomes fact, print the legend.'
John Ford hadn't quite finished with Stewart once
shooting on *The Man Who Shot Liberty Valance* came to an
end. During the filming of his final epic western *Cheyenne
Autumn* he called and said he had a part for him. Stewart
wondered just how he would fit into a tale of the long

flight of 300 Cheyenne from an Oklahoma reservation to their ancestral lands in the Dakota mountains. The answer was that in the middle of the long, sometimes torturous 161 minutes Ford had included a fifteen-minute segment called 'The Battle of Dodge City'. Stewart was to play Wyatt Earp, and Arthur Kennedy, his old sparring partner from the Anthony Mann westerns, was cast as Doc Holliday. The segment had nothing to do with the main film and was treated as a piece of broad comedy.

No one has satisfactorily explained why the scene was included in the film. One theory was that the film was so long and unrelenting that something other than the usual ten minute interval (the norm for road show productions of the time) was needed to liven things up. Yet some theatres played the film with the sequence and others without. There were even some that included the scene *and* an intermission.

Irrelevant as it was, the episode seemed the best part of a long and turgid film. The reference books state that James Stewart made three films with John Ford. In truth, it was more like two and a half. Stewart's only regret was that he worked with the film-maker when he was obviously way past his best and in deteriorating health. He envied Wayne and Fonda in that they had worked with him when he was at his peak. But to work with him at all was a bonus. He remembered him fondly and always with a smile. Ford's tough, frequently cantankerous nature was forgotten in the end, even by Henry Fonda. Stewart said:

He was a hard-nosed director. He knew what he wanted and exactly where to put the camera. His motto was 'Don't let the actors talk unless they have something to say' ... He never talked about movies when he was resting between takes or taking a drink after a day's shooting. Just sport and baseball and sometimes his days in the navy.

He liked to get a scene on the first or second take. If he didn't, he felt the actors lost their spontaneity; they'd lose the sparkle and the uncertainty. He liked it if you weren't quite sure of your lines. I think he felt it gave the scene a sense of nervousness and suspense.

I think it was the front-office executives that he hated most. Someone told me of the occasion when someone complained on set that Ford was running over schedule. Ford simply picked up the script, tore out ten pages and said: 'Right, now we're back on schedule.' I can't say I ever saw him do that and it may be one of those Hollywood stories but I can believe he could have done it. He had a very short fuse.

As for Ford's feelings about James Stewart? As usual, he didn't waste words, but the words he did use were most appropriate. Chewing on his handkerchief and scowling at the damn fool journalist who had asked him the question, he said: 'People just liked him. He played himself but he played the character.'

18   The Last Westerns

'The vogue for the new kind of western
seems pretty unimportant to me.'
                                    James Stewart

The change in the western came about suddenly and it
came about because of Sergio Leone's *A Fistful of Dollars*, a
revenge tale about a stranger who cleans up a Mexican
border town. The star was Clint Eastwood who just ten
years earlier had watched Stewart making the Anthony
Mann westerns at Universal.

The opening scene vividly illustrated what was to
follow. Eastwood, teeth clenched hard on a cigarillo, stood
with his hands hovering by the gunholster partly
obscured by his poncho. He spoke softly: 'You gonna
apologize to my mules?' The four gunmen barring his way
gave no hint that they were going to apologize about
anything. Leering defiantly, they stood their ground.
Then, gunfire! Deafening and prolonged gunfire. The
gunmen dropped in their tracks in the dusty street.

Eastwood holstered his guns. He glanced up at the
pitiless sun then said casually: 'You'd better get those men
under the ground quickly.' Slowly, he sauntered away
from the carnage. The spaghetti western had arrived!

Stewart's reaction to all this was the same as most other
veteran western stars – shock, bewilderment and dismay.
At a stroke it seemed, Leone had undone all the hard work
of Ford and Hawks and Mann and taken the western back
to basics. Instead of the poetry of Ford, the macho realism
of Hawks and the splendour of Mann's genuine western
landscapes, there was a kind of pantomime, half comic,
half sadistic, full of squinting close-ups, crude violence

155

and locations that were laughably inept. The lease on the American western had run out. It had been taken up by the film-makers of Italy and Spain.

Veteran directors who for years had been filming in Arizona and New Mexico grumbled about the crudity of it all. The light was all wrong, they said. There were no storylines. Eastwood was simply blowing people away from one film to the next. The American critics also showed their distaste: 'A treat for necrophiliacs,' said Judith Crist. 'The rest of us can get our kicks for free at the butcher's store.'

Arthur Knight in *Saturday Review* commented: 'Crammed with sadism and a distaste for human values that would make the ordinary misanthrope seem like Pollyanna, the only possible excuse for these films is to make money. Somehow, that isn't enough.'

As Stewart and other western stars discovered, however, it *was* enough. Not for the first time had the critics and the industry misread public taste. The public revelled in the crudity, and they asked for more, and they asked for Eastwood in particular. For many he was the modern equivalent of Gary Cooper; for others he was the western counterpart of the James Bond anti-hero who had emerged in Britain just a couple of years earlier. In Italy, *A Fistful of Dollars* became the most successful Italian film ever made. Others quickly followed. Those starring Eastwood – *For a Few Dollars More, The Good, the Bad and the Ugly* – cleaned up at the box office.

The major side effect of this sudden transformation of the western was that the kind of western that had helped Stewart re-establish his career after the war had become old fashioned. Hollywood still made them, just as they had always done. They needed the product and they were easy to make. Now though, they looked stale, *passé* even. Tales about ageing gunfighters had had their day. So too had stories dealing with ranchers versus homesteaders and battles for Indian territories. Only Sam Peckinpah with *The Wild Bunch* and George Roy Hill with *Butch Cassidy and the Sundance Kid* managed to find something new to say about the American West as they explored the twilight years of outlaws living in the early days of the twentieth century.

Stewart and company also found unexpected competition from actors who in American cinema had previously only been supporting players. Eli Wallach became a star when Leone asked for his services. Charles Bronson and Lee Van Cleef were two more who found fame when they ventured into spaghetti land. Van Cleef had been knocking around Hollywood for years and in 1962 had been fifteenth in the cast list of *The Man Who Shot Liberty Valance*. Four years later, when Ford directed his last film, *Seven Women*, Van Cleef achieved stardom in *For a Few Dollars More*.

Stewart was loathe to let the traditional western go. He said: 'If a western is a good western it gives you a sense of that world, and some of the qualities those men had – their comradeship, loyalty and physical courage. The vogue for the new kind of western seems pretty unimportant to me. They try to destroy something that has been vital to people for so long.'

Many echoed his views; a few believed that the traditional western was not dead and that the European imitation was no more than a flash in the pan. Others saw the truth. Stewart made his share of westerns in the mid sixties, among them *The Rare Breed, Bandolero* and *Shenandoah*. He also made a series of comedies at Fox. In the latter he was usually an absent-minded professor or a harassed father. In all of them he struggled with inferior material.

Even the westerns were routine, mostly rehashes of what had been filmed before. Only Andrew V. McLaglen's *Shenandoah* offered him the opportunity to prove that at fifty-seven he was still capable of great things as an actor. He was superb as a patriarchal farmer who is reluctantly drawn into the Civil War when one of his sons is kidnapped by the Unionists. He received fine notices and found himself briefly reinstated to the list of the top money-making stars in America. As the decade wore on, however, Stewart became uncomfortably aware of the fact that, for the first time since achieving stardom in the late thirties, he was no longer at the centre of things in Hollywood. He was on the periphery, looking in. Age of course had a lot to do with it. Also the demise of the traditional western. But the main reason was that the Hollywood he had known for thirty years was on shifting sands. The moguls had gone – at least most of them had. DeMille no longer strode the lot at Paramount. There were no longer any long-term contracts. The cameramen, the editors and technicians who had once been on a studio payroll for life now freelanced as the studios relied more and more on releasing independently made productions.

Also the character of the studios was no longer in evidence. One studio seemed very much like another. They had always been referred to as 'factories' but there had at least been some individual style to their product. Now there was none. Stewart saw at first hand how much things had changed when Darryl F. Zanuck called him in to make an innocuous little comedy called *Take Her She's Mine*. It was the first picture put into production on the Fox lot since the Elizabeth Taylor/Richard Burton disaster *Cleopatra* had brought the studio to its knees and caused it to cease production for nine months.

The Fox Stewart saw on his return to the studio was a much changed and leaner outfit. The backlot had been reduced from 280 acres to a more manageable 76 acres. The staff had been trimmed to a minimum. Many of the studio's vast stages stood empty and unused. Ghosts of Tyrone Power and Betty Grable and Alice Faye seemed to lurk around every corner. To Stewart's eyes it was a sorry sight.

His most sensible option at this stage of his career would have been to have cut the size of his roles and opt instead for character parts. In Europe, James Mason, an actor of the same age had found himself in a similar situation and accepted smaller roles even though his name was not above the title. With parts in *Lord Jim, Georgy Girl* and *The Pumpkin Eater*, he began a whole new career for himself. The only character role that came Stewart's way, however, was that of pilot Frank Towne in Robert Aldrich's *Flight of the Phoenix*. The film was an Elleston Trevor tale about an old twin-engine plane that crashes in the Sahara and has to be rebuilt by its passengers so that they can escape certain death in the desert sun. Stewart's performance as the grizzled, disillusioned pilot indicated how good a character actor he might have become if given half the chance. But despite a strong, all-star male cast that included Richard Attenborough, Peter Finch, Ernest Borgnine and Hardy Kruger, the film was not a box-office success. Its 147 minutes turned out to be something of an endurance test for audiences.

So, with Hollywood pouring millions of dollars into lavish screen versions of stage musicals (none of which offered Stewart any opportunities whatsoever) and thriving on small independent productions like *Easy Rider* (which offered him even less) Stewart ended the decade as he had begun – making westerns.

Two of them co-starred Hank Fonda with whom he hadn't worked since *On Our Merry Way* back in 1948. The first, *Firecreek*, was a routine affair with Stewart as the part-time sheriff of a small township and Fonda as the leader of a gang of outlaws that threatens the town. It was turgid, sub-standard *High Noon* stuff. The public had seen it all before and weren't particularly interested in seeing it again. The second picture, *The Cheyenne Social Club* was a much livelier piece, a light-hearted romp about an itinerant cowpoke (Stewart) who inherits a boarding house – in reality a bordello – and together with his buddy (Fonda) rides West to claim his inheritance.

Gene Kelly was hired to direct. He had never directed a western before, but had just finished the exhausting and bad-tempered *Hello Dolly* at Fox so he was willing to try anything.

At first Fonda refused the movie. He said: 'I don't want to do it Jimmy. My part's too small. All I do is follow you around. There's no balance. You do all the talking.' Stewart was unwilling to make the movie without him. He assured him he'd fix it. He got in touch with the film's writer James Lee Barrett. Stewart said:

> I told him that Fonda had complained and that he really didn't talk enough.
>
> Jim said: 'Give me two days and I'll have it corrected.' Sure enough, two days later he sent me down the script. I knew his work well. It was always good so I didn't bother to look at it. I just sent it along to Hank. Hank called me up

and said: 'Well, that's more like it. Fine, when do we start?'

Later, I saw why he was so keen to get going. In the opening shot Hank and I go from Texas to Wyoming and Jim Barrett had Fonda talkin' the whole time. Every once in a while I'd stop and say: 'Do you realize that you've been talking for a hundred miles without stopping?' In the end, I get so fed up with it I tell him that if he doesn't shut up I'll shoot him.[1]

The Cheyenne Social Club was the last film in which Stewart used his horse Pie. Stewart had ridden him for twenty years in fifteen pictures and the horse was getting old. Normally he would have got through the movie had he been nursed gently and filming taken place at the normal altitude. But the film's location, Santa Fe, was 5,000ft. above sea level and after a few days the horse's breathing became laboured. Stewart refused to use him and called for a double instead. Stewart said:

It was terribly upsetting. I knew he was old and didn't have much longer to live. While we were up there Fonda began sketching him when I wasn't around. He was an excellent artist and later he painted a picture of Pie in watercolours. When we got home he brought the picture over. Two weeks later Pie died. It was a great loss. I really missed him after all those years. But the horse is still with me. I still have Hank's painting in the library.

Tragedy struck Stewart halfway through the shooting of *The Cheyenne Social Club* and a film that had promised to be a casual, pleasurable easy shoot, turned into a personal nightmare. He learned that his son Ronald had been killed in action in Vietnam.

Stewart had made three trips to Vietnam during the war. A Brigadier General on his retirement from the Air Force reserve in 1968, he had first visited on a B-52 mission from Guam to a target ten miles east of the Cambodian border. Later he made an inspection tour and finally a USO tour when he met the troops, visited hospitals and signed autographs.

It was on this final visit that, together with Gloria, he met up with his son who was in the Marines. He had been in action just south of the demilitarized zone in Quang Tri. Stewart never saw him again. Three months later he was killed.

Under the circumstances it was a miracle that Stewart managed to give any kind of performance at all. There were many days when he felt like quitting the picture altogether but he hung on, trying not to brood and let his mood affect the rest of the cast. On many occasions he found it impossible to sleep with the result that the next morning he would often be too tired to work. Gene Kelly had the unenviable task of holding things together. He said: 'I knew what he was suffering and whenever it happened I'd either shoot around him or cancel work for the day, depending on the schedule. And we'd all go fishing.'

Fonda did his best to raise Stewart's spirits by yarning about the old days and remembering the good times they had spent together. Stewart, momentarily brought out of his grief, responded with his own tales, like the time Fonda went to sleep on a bar in Mexico and awoke to find that John Wayne had wrapped a boa constrictor around his head!

Stewart was not sorry when shooting on *The Cheyenne Social Club* came to an end. In many ways he was also glad to see the back of the sixties. Compared with the previous decade it had not been an especially rewarding time professionally. A chance to work with John Ford, yes, that had been a plus, but there had been little else of note. Generally it had been a time when events had overtaken him, when the American cinema was suddenly no place for Jimmy Stewart. Producers no longer made Jimmy Stewart pictures. Instead, they made *Midnight Cowboy* and *Bonnie and Clyde* and *Bob and Carol and Ted and Alice*. It was, to all intents and purposes, a different world.

On a personal level the Vietnam War troubled him deeply. Always a Republican he had always supported American action but he expressed unhappiness about the way the country was divided. Those close to him said that after his son's death he was less vociferous than he had been before. He never expressed any public doubts but perhaps a few were there.

A year after Ronald's death Stewart said: 'Neither my wife nor I have any bitterness. We've gotten hundreds and hundreds of letters. I still believe in the cause he died for. The war has been a trial and a tremendously difficult thing for the nation. The tragedy is that there has been so much sacrifice without a unified nation behind the cause.'

As the sixties became the seventies Stewart said simply: 'I guess it's not too pleasant to be anywhere these days. It's not easy for me. But I still have faith in the country. I still think things will work out.'

Footnote

1. *Film Comment* (March–April, 1990)

19 Television

'The Jimmy Stewart Show is heavy with
integrity; and heavier with banality and
boredom.'

New York Times

It might have worked! A 65-year-old Stewart, a 66-year-old
Wayne and a 68-year-old Fonda – all in one film. They had
been together before, a decade earlier, in the Cinerama
spectacular *How The West Was Won* but like all the other
Hollywood stars in that western epic they had enjoyed
only cameo roles. Not once had they shared a single scene
together. Now, however, director Peter Bogdanovich
wanted them for the leads in his western *Streets of Laredo*.

Bogdanovich was one of the new young 'Brat Pack'
directors, but unlike Francis Ford Coppola and Martin
Scorsese and others his roots were firmly in the past. John
Ford and Howard Hawks were his heroes and it showed
in his films. His acclaimed *The Last Picture Show* looked at
life in a dying Texas town in the early fifties. His *Paper
Moon* was a lively Depression tale about conmen working
the Bible belt and *What's Up Doc* was a screwball comedy.
A western seemed the logical next step.

He lunched with Stewart to outline his idea. According
to Stewart that was all it was – an idea. 'We got along well
enough,' said Stewart, 'but we didn't seem to get
anywhere. It was all a bit hazy, everything was very much
in the 'it could happen if' stage. Nothing seemed definite.
But I was quite happy to consider it and said fine, go
ahead. Let's talk again when you've got a script.'

When Bogdanovich returned with a screenplay,
co-written by Larry McMurtry, who had written *The Last*

Picture Show and *Hud*, the result wasn't quite what Stewart had expected. Stewart said:

> I read it and I wasn't impressed. But I thought, well, perhaps it's me. So I called The Duke and asked him what he thought. He said: 'Jimmy boy, they're trying to make three old fogies out of us.' And he was right.
>
> I think all of us were disappointed in a way. I know Bogdanovich was. But the film didn't seem to have much of a story and it kept rubbing in our ages and declining powers. And we were pretty well aware of those anyway.

Stewart declined the film. So did Wayne and Fonda. Had he known that the Bogdanovich offer would be just about the only worthwhile role that would come his way in the seventies, Stewart's decision might have been different. On reflection, the movie might even have been fun. Bogdanovich was a hot director. He was on a roll. Further offers might have developed had it been a success, but the 'no' was firm and the picture was never made. All of which was a pity because it would almost certainly have done better business than *Fool's Parade*, the only seventies movie Stewart had made before *Streets of Laredo* came under discussion.

The picture was a Depression tale about an ex-jailbird (Stewart) who tries to set up a small store with the $25,000 he's saved in prison, but who constantly finds himself falling foul of crooked lawman George Kennedy. Andrew V. McLaglen directed and the film was another attempt by Stewart to play a character part even though he had the lead. He even wore a moustache and a glass eye for the role. Many critics liked the picture, but the public didn't. It flopped.

Compared with the films that were making big money in the early seventies, *Fool's Parade* was distinctly old hat. For most cinema managers it amounted to little more than a programme filler, something to play for a week until *A Clockwork Orange*, *Last Tango in Paris* or *Straw Dogs* came along. It seemed that all anyone wanted was sex, violence and pornography. Stewart was bewildered:

I just didn't seem to fit in anymore. Some of the scripts I was sent simply confused me.

I look at the theatre advertisements and I think, what have we got now. We've got violence. We've got films of an explosive nature. Then we've got films of a depressing nature. There's nothing else. The comedies have gone. There's no entertainment. There's no choice anymore.

The trouble is the movies they're making are the wrong kind of movies, seamy, hopeless, semi-pornographic things. At this point why should I fool around with stuff like that?

All of which meant that Stewart's options were, to say the least, limited. He could either branch out into other entertainment forms such as live theatre or television or he could retire gracefully. Some of the stars he had known and worked with over the years had already done so. Cagney had called it a day in 1961. Robert Montgomery, a survivor of the MGM days, had said enough was enough and so too had Cary Grant. In 1966 he had retired at the age of sixty-two to concentrate on his business interests. All could sense the way the wind was blowing. The modern cinema was no place for any of them.

Stewart could easily have done the same. A wealthy man, he could have spent his days lazing on the golf course or flying over Burbank in the little Super Cub plane he'd purchased at the end of the sixties. But even as he approached his seventies the 'excitement' of the movies was still with him. He still enjoyed the infectious activity on a movie set. He relished the enthusiasm and expectation on the first day of shooting and the thrill when the adrenalin was going in a really big scene. On the Dickensian assumption that something would eventually turn up he refused to contemplate retirement.

Instead, and rather than sit at home 'talking to the dog' he sought refuge with an old friend. He took *Harvey* back to the New York stage and even filmed it once more, this time for television, opposite Helen Hayes. In 1975 he took the play to London. The critics were as enthusiastic as they had been in America. That actors such as Harold Lloyd, Joe E. Brown, Jack Buchanan, Sid Fields and Rudy

Vallee had all, at one time in their careers, played Elwood P. Dowd, was forgotten. Stewart's 'Elwood P.' was as inseparable from his own persona as Rex Harrison's Professor Higgins in *My Fair Lady*, Yul Brynner's King Tut in *The King and I* and Anthony Quinn's fun-loving eccentric in *Zorba The Greek*.

Variety said of his Broadway return in *Harvey*: 'He's a genuine star, with the presence, projection, feel of an audience and the personal magnetism to take command of a theatre. He gives the impression of almost not acting at all.' *The New York Daily News* concurred: 'Stewart offers a master class of acting with each performance.'

Stewart's experience with television on the other hand was much less successful. He had never been over-impressed with the medium. It had always seemed second, even third best to the cinema. He had guested occasionally on *The Jack Benny Show* and even, sporadically, acted in the medium. In 1955 he had played a poverty-stricken rancher in the thirty-minute TV film *The Windmill* and in 1962 he appeared for John Ford in *Flashing Spikes*, the story of the ball-player Slim Conway. He even directed a western version of *A Christmas Carol*, called *Trail To Christmas*, but that's as far as it went.

Generally, he tended to go along with Billy Wilder's description of the small screen: 'I think TV is great. Now we in the movies have something to look down on.'

Stewart made two ventures into television in the early 70s. The first was entitled simply *The Jimmy Stewart Show* and was no more than a thirty-minute sitcom about the family squabbles of a small-town anthropology professor. Stewart's idiot father, full of the usual wide-eyed mannerisms, was required to cope weekly with all manner of relatives and grandchildren. It was all harmless enough of its kind, but hardly of the stature to show off the talents of Stewart at his best. Said the *New York Times*: 'The show is heavy with integrity; and heavier with banality and boredom.'

Stewart later complained about the lack of planning of the entire venture. There was no pilot. Everything was hit or miss. One story had it that when NBC executives met with Stewart to ask him what the show was about he replied: 'About half an hour.' Uncharacteristically, Stewart withdrew into his shell. He even refused all interviews. Later, he told a Hollywood correspondent: 'The trouble was I had too much authority. And I made too many errors. I was given the approval of all the characters, the scripts, the shooting schedules. It just didn't work. People should stick to what they do well. I'm an actor. Someone else should have been calling the shots.'

The second venture, made during 1973–74, was a much better organized affair. Called *Hawkins* the series cast Stewart as a down-to-earth West Virginia lawyer and drew heavily on his performance as Paul Biegler in *Anatomy of a Murder*. The eight ninety-minute shows were well scripted and efficiently made. They even earned Stewart a Golden Globe for his acting. But when one came right down to it, it was still a case of 'we've been here before', ten years ago with Otto Preminger. And then things had been really classy. *Hawkins* was good television, but had it been shown on the big screen it would have amounted to no more than average entertainment.

In all eight of the *Hawkins* films Stewart defended his client. He never prosecuted. His cases ranged from the murder of a homosexual to the killing of a movie producer, from the killing of a computer analyst to a triple murder supposedly committed by an heiress. He said: 'When the facts were against me I argued the law. When the law was against me I argued the facts. And when the facts and the law were against me I banged my hands on the table. The formula seemed to work – convincing on TV at least.'

It was the hectic pace of television and the intense learning of lines that eventually caused Stewart to call it a day on *Hawkins*. He could never quite get accustomed to the speed at which TV directors worked or that one take, or at best, two, was all that was needed. It was 'one take, cut, print'. He admitted that he had trouble memorizing the scripts in the time allotted to him. When someone gently pointed out that it would be quite in order for him to use cue cards he replied: 'That won't work. I can't *see* the cue cards.'

The most depressing thing about *Hawkins* was that it was shot at his old home studio of MGM, or rather at the remains of MGM. It was a case of Stewart's career coming full circle. Memories of his first day at Culver City in the summer of 1935 came flooding back. Then the place had been buzzing, vibrant, alive with movies rolling off the lot at four a month. Now it was a wasteland, dilapidated, no longer a force to be reckoned with.

The paint peeled from the 'star' dressing rooms. The backlot and the outdoor stages had fallen into disrepair, rusting, overgrown, unkempt. The once magnificent main street that had been used to film movies like *Meet Me In St Louis* had become shabby, retaining none of its former splendour. The train station where Fred Astaire had first alighted in *The Band Wagon* was run down. It was difficult not to recall how grand things had once been. When, in 1974, Stewart was selected as one of the eight hosts for Metro's musical extravaganza *That's Entertainment*, the decline became even more evident.

The return made Stewart realize the value of the studio system even more. The studios had been his life. He missed the well-oiled studio machines, the camaraderie of his fellow actors, even the tantrums of the moguls.

Above all he envied the stars of old. For them there had been the safety of employment. Many had carried on well into their seventies, even their eighties. He remembered Leon Ames, Wallace Beery, Louis Calhern and the silent screen veteran Lewis Stone who was still appearing in five character roles a year when he was seventy-two. His old friend Lionel Barrymore with whom he had spent many happy hours had been another long term survivor and had still been before the cameras at Metro when he was seventy-five.

Now, it seemed, Hollywood had turned into a hustler's paradise. It wasn't a term that Stewart liked to use, but it was one that was heard frequently around Hollywood in the seventies. By the end of the decade, Stewart was to all intents and purposes, a forgotten star, yesterday's man. Much loved whenever he made personal appearances or was a guest of honour at functions, he was, nonetheless, a man who was known to the younger generation only by his old movies which played regularly on TV.

He appeared in just four films after *Fool's Parade*. In 1976 he shared a few scenes with Duke Wayne in *The Shootist*, as the doctor who has to tell the ageing gunfighter that he is dying of cancer. A year later came another cameo as a wealthy art collector in the all-star disaster movie *Airport 77*. In 1978 he visited Britain to appear as the dying General Sternwood in Michael Winner's ludicrous remake of Raymond Chandler's *The Big Sleep*. Then in 1981, came *The Magic of Lassie* in which he featured as a Californian vineyard owner – and a grandfather.

Stewart defended the last named film saying that he made it because it was one of the few films around that had any moral integrity. He even croaked a couple of numbers on his accordion. The image of a once great star reduced to this was not a pleasing one.

Then, out of the blue, came the call from The American Film Institute ...

20   Hollywood 1980

'With any kind of Capra luck you're
going to make my children's children
very happy.'

Dustin Hoffman

At the Beverly Hills Hilton the celebrations of the
American Film Institute continued.

The tributes came from friends and former co-stars. One
by one they stood by their tables to offer an anecdote of
what it was like to have worked on a Jimmy Stewart
picture.

Richard Widmark said a few words about the western
Two Rode Together. George Kennedy remembered *Bandolero*. The lovable veteran Beulah Bondi spoke of playing
Stewart's mother five times in movies and on TV. Director
Henry Hathaway recalled *Call Northside 777*. Then there
was Ruth Hussey, Karl Malden, Ernest Borgnine, director
Mervyn LeRoy, Douglas Morrow who thanked Stewart on
behalf of the writers.

Then, of course, there was Capra, a diminutive figure,
natty and smart, who came to the podium to a standing
ovation and spoke warmly of the actor with whom he had
worked so memorably on three occasions. He said:

There is a higher level than great performances in acting. A
level where there is no acting at all. The actor disappears
and there's only a real live person on the screen. A person
audiences care about immediately. There are only a few
actors, very few, capable of achieving this highest level of
the actor's art. And that tall stringbean sitting right over
there, he's one of them. Thank you very much.

Stewart, his eyes moist, stood with the rest of the gathering as Capra left the stage. Everything that happened on that February night in 1980 was sincere and deeply felt. It was also expected. People anticipated that Jack Lemmon would come to the mike and after a series of Stewart imitations say 'You're a great actor sir.' They anticipated too the kind words of Grace Kelly and the others who stood in line to have their say.

What they did not expect was the appearance of the young Dustin Hoffman, then forty-three and about to win his first Oscar for his harassed father in *Kramer vs. Kramer*. A kind of surprised 'What is he doing here?' buzz went around the room. Hoffman, nervous and slightly fumbling, stood on his own by the microphone. He said:

> The truth of the matter is Mr Stewart, I wanted to be here tonight to see a lot of your work and to hear people talk about you, people I've never met, and hear stories I've never heard. My father grew up with you. My father worked on the lot when you were making Mr Capra's *Mr Smith Goes to Washington* and he's your age.

Hoffman paused to break the tension, adding with a shy smile and much to the audience's delight: 'My mother is my age and that's one of my problems!' As the laughter subsided he continued:

> I saw *It's a Wonderful Life* two days ago for the first time. I think I'm maybe the only one here to have seen it recently. It's a great, great film and a great piece of work and you could have shown it tonight and it would have been a tribute in itself. I congratulate you for a really first-class piece of work sir.

Stewart, as surprised as everyone else in the room at this turn of events, smiled and nodded his appreciation.

Hoffman, though was not finished:

> I'm the only one up here representing my generation of actors ... When I saw you on screen in that performance you made me laugh, you made me cry and you made me wish for a country which perhaps we haven't seen for a

while. I was told that *It's a Wonderful Life* was not a success, that you came back from the Second World War and made this film and were told by critics and people in this town that your career was at a low ebb and that you were down and out. I was also told that you'd made the comment that you weren't sure whether you were an unemployed actor or an unemployed flier.

Well, let me just say in closing that you made my parents very happy, you have made me very happy and that I'm sure you're going to make my children very happy. And if this world has any Capra luck you're going to make my children's children very happy.

Hoffman's tribute was the hit of the evening. It came from the heart, it was delivered to perfection and it caught the mood perfectly. Nothing that followed came anywhere near to topping it.

As the evening drew to its climax, American Film Institute chairman George Stevens, jun., beckoned for Stewart to come to accept his award. The years had been rolled back, the life examined, the films explored. There was no nervousness about Stewart's performance at the podium. Instead, there was a wry, self-deprecating humour as he played for real the James Stewart everyone had known for years.

Thank you all for sharing such a wonderful evening which is about to go downhill fast as I fumble around for the right words to express my appreciation. I know it's late and I promised myself to talk fast so as not to keep you up any later than is necessary. The problem is I don't know *how* to talk fast.

I guess you could say that, until tonight, the American Film Institute has honoured brilliance, daring, abundance of talent and attainment of the highest ideals of the motion picture community and that, er, brings us down to where we are now.

He lingered over the next words, giving a Capra-like emphasis to their meaning. 'When the American Film Institute in all its *wisdom*, adds a new name and a new category to the Life Achievement Award – Jimmy Stewart, a remarkably fortunate fella.' Stewart waved, the cameras flashed, the crowd stood. The evening was over.

21   Little Pieces of Time

'My job has been my life. I never ever
thought about retiring. To walk away
from it wouldn't seem fair somehow.'

James Stewart

The eighties were a winding down time for Stewart, a time
when he found himself exchanging the role of actor for
that of a new role – a roving elder statesman-cum-
ambassador for the film world.

Some scripts did still come his way, but they were few
and far between. He read about three or four a month. He
smiled ruefully and said:

Grandfathers, that's all I seem to get sent. I know the age
thing is important and I guess I can't expect much else, but
now, whenever I see a script and see that the character is
introduced as 'a grouchy old man', I slam the script shut
and send it back. It puzzles me why they think that just
because you're old you have to be grouchy. I refuse to play
grouchy old men.

The passing of old friends further dampened his spirits.
Leland Hayward was no longer around to chew over old
times. 'Duke' Wayne had also gone, aged seventy-two,
from cancer. So too had Hitch and Hank Fonda and, most
tragically of all, Grace Kelly who, at fifty-two, had fallen
victim to the treacherous roads that wind their way high
above Monaco.

There was at least the occasional TV work to keep him
in front of the cameras. He was fond of a short film he
made called *Mr Krueger's Christmas* in which he played a
lonely janitor living out his fantasy as the conductor of

The Mormon Tabernacle Choir. He was delighted when he found himself starring, for the first time in his career, with Bette Davis in a 1983 TV movie called *Right of Way*. Davis, then seventy-five, was as short of work as he was and leapt at the chance of playing opposite a man who, despite all the studio loan-outs and innumerable star teamings over the years, had never been cast opposite her.

Both stars were especially grateful for the chance to appear in leading roles once more and also to feature in something that was meaningful. Both felt the film to be important, dealing as it did with old age and a suicide pact made between a husband and wife when the wife discovers she is dying of an incurable blood disease. No doubt there was a feeling among the producers that if *On Golden Pond* which had also focused on old age and earned Oscars for Henry Fonda and Katharine Hepburn, could achieve success on the big screen, there was no reason why *Right of Way* should not enjoy a similar triumph on television.

Unfortunately, things didn't quite work out that way. Despite sensitive direction from George Schaefer and deeply felt performances from its two stars *Right of Way* was only a limited success. Most critics admired the acting, but found the film worthy and admirable rather than enjoyable. Not surprisingly in view of the subject matter, audiences also found it frequently depressing.

Still, the actual filming was fun. It reminded Stewart and Davis of the old days. The budget was tiny, just $2.8 million. There was no time for location work. The picture was completed in just twenty days. It wasn't quite like being back at Warners or Paramount, but both stars enjoyed the speed and professionalism with which the film (the first to be made expressly for cable television) was put together.

The fact that they were working with each other for the first time also helped. Said Stewart: 'I never thought I would get to work with her. I thought she was one of those that I'd miss. When I started at MGM she was at Warners and Warners just didn't loan out Bette to other studios. She was at the top. Working with her was exhilarating from the first day to the last.'

For her part Davis was almost coquettish: 'I felt I had known him for years. I wish I had met him when I was younger. I most definitely would have fallen in love with him.' She chuckled. 'I told him this. He just gave me one of those Stewart "slow-take" looks.'

Davis wasn't the only one who had nice things to say about James Stewart in the eighties. So frequent were the tributes and retrospectives of his work that Stewart found himself having to find different ways of saying a humble 'thank you' for the effusive praise that came his way from all over the world.

In 1982 he was fêted at the Berlin Film Festival for his contribution to the cinema and in 1983 he was one of the honorees, along with Frank Sinatra, Elia Kazan, Virgil Thomson and Katharine Dunham, at the Kennedy Centre in Washington. The same year came an honour and celebration that gave him particular satisfaction, one held in his home town of Indiana, Pennsylvania on the occasion of his seventy-fifth birthday. There were three days of events including a film festival, the presenting of a huge birthday cake and the unveiling of a 9ft. statue.

The Oscars too had not finished with him. In March 1985, the Academy presented him with a special award: 'For his fifty years of memorable performances. For his high ideals both on and off the screen. With the respect and affection of his colleagues.' The award was presented by Cary Grant.

Two months later the Cannes Film Festival also showed its appreciation, presenting a special homage to Stewart and accompanying it with a unique showing of a newly restored print of *The Glenn Miller Story*. There was even a trip to Rio to help re-promote four of his Hitchcock films which had been out of circulation for several years and were about to enjoy a new life in the cinema and on television.

He was, in every way, the perfect Hollywood ambassador, a cinematic elder statesman who in many ways did more for Hollywood's image than the stars whose names were then above the titles of the latest movies. Still eager in his late seventies to enjoy the enthusiasm of young people to whom he was something of a legend, he continued to spin (and enlarge) his tales of Hitchcock, Capra and the rest. Autographs were frequently requested and never refused. Always his speeches were grateful, sincere, full of humility and genuine. There was never an ounce of hypocrisy about him.

There were things he railed against. The colourization of old black and white movies was one. It especially hurt him when his own favourite film, *It's a Wonderful Life* became the first victim of the process. He said:

> They did it because it went into public domain, I saw about just two minutes of it and I got just sick.
>
> They don't seem to realize that films are a piece of property, that they were made by a director, a cameraman and a team of technicians. I feel worse about it for them than anyone else especially when I think about the time that it took them for the lighting, to get depth to the scene. Colourization takes all the shadows out; everything. They're gone. And everyone has a light brown face. It's wrong.
>
> I still get quite a bit of fan mail and they all agree with me. They should leave it alone.

About video he is more enthusiastic. In May, 1990 he showed up at a West Los Angeles video store to promote an MCA-Universal release of *Harvey* which included a six-minute introduction by Stewart himself. He was grateful that the tape was in the original black and white. Seven hundred fans turned up at the store paying out nearly $20 a time to own a copy of the 1950 picture about Elwood P. Dowd and his invisible, floppy-eared friend.

Prior to the release of *Harvey* only health and fitness videos had received the star treatment when it came to promotion. Stewart, however, became the first actor to help promote a *movie* on tape even though his appearance was strictly a one-off occasion. The store owner, Tom Trainer and his wife Maria were friends of the Stewarts. Said Trainer: 'I saw *Harvey* was coming out and I thought it would be great if we could get Jimmy in the store. It was a big success.'

Asked about the state of the modern cinema Stewart finds himself unable to offer anything different to what he had said a decade earlier:

> I don't want to keep sounding as though I wanna go back to the good old days. That's a kind of cop-out. But it's still the lack of variety that depresses me. There's a place for everything. Even the strong, adult movies. Some of 'em are good. But the medium has a tremendous capacity and it should be exploited more.
>
> You get porno, sex, violence. The pictures are cynical and they all seem to be alike. It's hard to find a movie where you can just enjoy yourself, yet there used to be so many of them. Like everyone else, I have problems of my own; I don't want to go to a movie that dumps into my lap someone else's imaginary problems.

What about his acting style? The mere suggestion or hint that he always played himself will bring about the closest you will get to irritation from Jimmy Stewart.

A natural actor then?

> No, I'm sorry but that is not an accurate way of describing what I do. I act but I try not to let it show. The idea is to be so persuasive that people believe what you're doing is actually real. There aren't any rules or methods I follow except for a few little experimentations and a few physical tricks. If you get people believing in what you're doing then you are in pretty good shape.

> One of the things that has helped me is that I've always felt from people that they've had a friendly attitude, which has been very nice. Geez, they say, I *know* that fellow ... you can feel the concern, the friendliness. They come up and say: 'I feel I *know* you.' Some of it has resulted from the kind of parts I've been in. But the important thing is that they should be concerned for your welfare up there on the screen. 'Cause I've always felt through the years that although they're always quite sure that everything will come out right with most actors – they're nawt quite sure in my case.

His biggest disappointment of recent times?

Giving up flying I guess. I loved the Piper Cub that I used
to own. I used to go out every week taking the little thing
up into the mountains and landing at tiny strips the
ranchers had laid down. But I had a hearing problem and it
got so that I couldn't understand communications from the
tower I would have to have them repeat everything.

Then I tried putting a loudspeaker in the plane. Only
trouble was they could hear me all over the airport but I
couldn't understand a thing. So, I just had to give it up. I
miss it terribly. But I had it for forty-five years. I guess
that's long enough. I had a pretty good run.'

Anything else he misses. What about the studios?

Yeah, I do miss them, especially Metro. It was a shame
when they went into decline. The moguls you know
weren't anywhere near as bad as they've been painted.
They *knew* film, they really did, they *smelt* film, and people
learned about making movies. In those days you learned a
lot about movies, not by reading, not by going to lectures,
but by doing the job.

The actor he would most liked to have worked with?

[Pause. Slow drawl] Cagney, I guess. [A wry smile.] That
would have been interesting don't you think ... Yeah
Cagney and Bogart.

Actresses?

Waal, I guess I worked with most of the girls. [Another
pause] There was really only Bette and we did get together
at the end.

Directors?

I was so lucky. I worked with the best. I really did. Capra,
Hitchcock, Stevens, Cukor and Preminger of course, and
Jack Ford. They all seemed to want me in their pictures.
Willie Wyler I missed out on. We never seemed to get
together. One thing I do know is that all of them asked me

to talk faster. Mr Hitchcock had a slightly different way of telling me. He used to take me aside after a shot and say: 'Jim, the scene is tired.'

Regrets?

Perhaps I should have spent more time on the stage. I always admired my friend Hank Fonda for putting aside time between films to return to the theatre. But apart from that, nothing. It really has been a wonderful life. My job has been my life. I never ever thought about retiring. To walk away from it wouldn't seem fair somehow.

Today, he lives a happy, tranquil life. He still lives in the same house to which he moved after marrying Gloria in 1949. His daughters and son are married with children. He is a grandfather several times over. He tends his garden, goes to church, remains keenly interested in animal preservation, especially in Africa, and has whiled away the last few years with the occasional appearance on TV chat shows, reading a script or two, even writing a book of poetry. In the Spring of 1990 he attended yet another salute to his career and work at Lincoln Center, New York. The evening was a sell-out.

Quite whether he sees many movies these days is doubtful. But despite the graphic violence of today's cinema he has never lost interest in the medium he served and which, as he is the first to admit, served him so well for so many years.

He never fails to retell a favourite anecdote which he feels demonstrates more than anything else the importance of the movies on people's lives in the twentieth century. He says:

I remember we were up in Canada, in 1954, in the mountains shooting a picture called *The Far Country*. We were having a box lunch – the usual terrible box lunch – and this old guy came into the camp, looked around, saw me, came over, nodded. 'You Stewart?'

'Yeah.'

'You did a thing in a picture once,' he said. 'Can't remember the name of it but you were in a room and you said a poem or something about fireflies – that was good.'

I knew right away what he meant. That's all he said. He was talking about a scene in a picture called *Come Live With Me* that came out in 1941, and he couldn't remember the title. But that little thing – didn't even last a minute – he'd remembered all those years. And *that's* the thing, that's the great thing about the movies. If you're good and God helps you and you're lucky enough to have a personality that comes across, you're giving people little, little tiny pieces of time – pieces of time that they never forget.

Jimmy Stewart is I think, assured of his wish. Those little pieces of time are preserved forever in mint condition in the archives of The American Film Institute. His films may grow older by the year, but in every one, and it is no exaggeration to say *every* one, there is a moment, sometimes more than one, that remains clearly etched on one's memory:

Stewart, grabbing nervously for his flashbulbs to photograph and temporarily blind the lumbering killer Raymond Burr in *Rear Window*.

Quivering with excitement as he helps to enlarge the type of an old newspaper date and proves the innocence of Richard Conte in *Call Northside 777*.

Waltzing, intoxicated round a swimming pool with Katharine Hepburn in *The Philadelphia Story*.

Holding the dying Dietrich in his arms in *Destry Rides Again*.

Praying and near to tears as he sits at a bar and contemplates suicide in *It's a Wonderful Life*.

Reacting, wide-eyed and innocent and stumbling awkwardly for words as Lee Remick lounges back on a sofa and informs him that he's interested in her sexually in *Anatomy of a Murder*.

Riding silently and alone into an Apache stronghold in *Broken Arrow*.

Imploring Kim Novak to complete the transformation and become the perfect reproduction of the woman he loved and lost in *Vertigo*.

Kneeling by his wife's grave in *Shenandoah* and trying to rid himself of the Civil War that is engulfing him: 'I don't even know what to say to you Martha. There's nothing much I can tell you about this war. It's ... it's like all wars I suppose. The undertakers are winning it. Politicians talk a lot about the glory of it. Soldiers? They just want to go home.'

There are so many moments in all of Stewart's films. In more than eighty movies he has made audiences believe that he was a professor, a soldier, a reporter, a lawyer, a bandleader, a sheriff, an aviator, a senator, a lover, a tippler, a family man. Always he has been American, but always he has been vulnerable. Idealistic but stubborn. Awkward but graceful.

His is a rich heritage. As Dustin Hoffman might say, our children's children have much to discover and enjoy and appreciate.

Filmography

MURDER MAN (1935)
MGM: 70 minutes
Producer: Harry Rapf. *Director*: Tim Whelan. *Screenplay*: Tim Whelan and John C. Higgins, based on a story by Whelan and Guy Bolton. *Photography*: Lester White. *Music*: William Axt. *Leading players*: Spencer Tracy, Virginia Bruce, Lionel Atwill, Harvey Stephens, Robert Barrat, James Stewart (as Shorty), William Collier Sr., Bobby Watson, William Demarest.
Released: July 1935.

ROSE MARIE (1936)
MGM: 113 minutes
Producer: Hunt Stromberg. *Director*: W.S. Van Dyke II. *Screenplay*: Frances Goodrich, Albert Hackett and Alice Duer Miller, based on the musical play by Otto Harbach and Oscar Hammerstein II. *Photography*: William Daniels. *Music*: Rudolf Friml and Herbert Stothart. *Leading players*: Jeanette MacDonald, Nelson Eddy, James Stewart, Reginald Owen, Allan Jones, George Regas, Robert Greig, Gilda Gray, Una O'Connor, Lucien Littlefield, Alan Mowbray, David Niven.
Released: January 1936.

NEXT TIME WE LOVE (1936)
Universal: 87 minutes
Producer: Paul Kohner. *Director*: Edward H. Griffith. *Screenplay*: Melville Baker, based on the story 'Say Goodbye Again' by Ursula Parrott. *Photography*: Joseph Valentine. *Music*: Franz Waxman. *Leading players*: Margaret Sullavan, James Stewart, Ray Milland, Anna Demetrio, Grant Mitchell, Robert McWade, Ronnie Cosbey, Florence Roberts, Christian Rub.
Released: January 1936.

WIFE VS. SECRETARY (1936)
MGM: 88 minutes
Producer: Hunt Stromberg. *Director*: Clarence Brown. *Screenplay*: Norman Krasna, Alice Duer Miller and John Lee Mahin, based on the story by Faith Baldwin. *Photography*: Ray June. *Music*: Herbert Stothart. *Leading players*: Clark Gable, Jean Harlow, Myrna Loy, May Robson,

Hobart Cavanaugh, James Stewart, George Barbier, Gilbert Emery, Margaret Irving.
Released: February 1936.

SMALL TOWN GIRL (1936)
MGM: 90 minutes
Producer: Hunt Stromberg. *Director*: William A. Wellman. *Screenplay*: John Lee Mahin, based on the novel by Ben Ames Williams. *Photography*: Charles Rosher. *Music*: Herbert Stothart. *Leading players*: Janet Gaynor, Robert Taylor, Binnie Barnes, James Stewart, Lewis Stone, Elizabeth Patterson, Frank Craven, Andy Devine, Isabel Jewell, Charley Grapewin, Agnes Ayres.
Released: April 1936.

SPEED (1936)
MGM: 65 minutes
Producer: Lucien Hubbard. *Director*: Edwin L. Marin. *Screenplay*: Michael Fessier, based on a story by Milton Krims and Larry Bachman. *Photography*: Lester White. *Music*: Edward Ward. *Leading players*: James Stewart, Wendy Barrie, Ted Healy, Una Merkel, Weldon Heyburne, Patricia Wilder, Ralph Morgan.
Released: May 1936.

THE GORGEOUS HUSSY (1936)
MGM: 102 minutes
Producer: Joseph L. Mankiewicz. *Director*: Clarence Brown. *Screenplay*: Ainsworth Morgan and Stephen Morehouse, based on a story by Samuel Hopkins Adams. *Photography*: George Folsey. *Music*: Herbert Stothart. *Leading players*: Joan Crawford, Robert Taylor, Lionel Barrymore, Melvyn Douglas, Franchot Tone, James Stewart, Louis Calhern, Alison Skipworth, Beulah Bondi, Melville Cooper.
Released: September 1936.

BORN TO DANCE (1936)
MGM: 108 minutes
Producer: Jack Cummings. *Director*: Roy Del Ruth. *Screenplay*: Jack McGowan, Sid Silvers and B.G. De Sylva. *Photography*: Ray June. *Songs*: Cole Porter. *Music Director*: Alfred Newman. *Leading players*: Eleanor Powell, James Stewart, Virginia Bruce, Una Merkel, Sid Silvers, Frances Langford, Raymond Walburn, Alan Dinehart.
Released: November 1936.

AFTER THE THIN MAN (1936)
MGM: 110 minutes
Producer: Hunt Stromberg. *Director*: W.S. Van Dyke II. *Screenplay*: Frances Goodrich and Albert Hackett, based on a story by Dashiell Hammett. *Photography*: Oliver T. Marsh. *Music*: Herbert Stothart. *Leading players*: Myrna Loy, William Powell, James Stewart, Elissa Landi, Joseph Calleia, Jessie Ralph, Alan Marshall, Sam Levene.
Released: December 1936.

SEVENTH HEAVEN (1937)
20th Century-Fox: 102 minutes
Producer: Darryl F. Zanuck. *Director*: Henry King. *Screenplay*: Melville Baker, based on the play by Austin Strong. *Photography*: Merritt Gerstad. *Music Direction*: Louis Silvers. *Leading players*: Simone Simon, James Stewart, Gale Sondergaard, Gregory Ratoff, Jean Hersholt, J. Edward Bromberg, Victor Kilian, John Qualen, Mady Christians, Sig Rumann.
Released: March 1937.

THE LAST GANGSTER (1937)
MGM: 81 minutes
Producer: J.J. Cohn. *Director*: Edward Ludwig. *Screenplay*: John Lee Mahin, from a story by William A. Wellman and Robert Carson. *Photography*: William Daniels. *Music*: Edward Ward. *Leading players*: Edward G. Robinson, James Stewart, Rose Stradner, Lionel Stander, Douglas Scott, John Carradine, Sidney Blackmer, Grant Mitchell, Edward Brophy, Alan Baxter.
Released: November 1937.

NAVY BLUE AND GOLD (1937)
MGM: 94 minutes
Producer: Sam Zimbalist. *Director*: Sam Wood. *Screenplay*: George Bruce, based on his novel. *Photography*: John Seitz. *Music*: Edward Ward. *Leading players*: Robert Young, James Stewart, Lionel Barrymore, Florence Rice, Billie Burke, Tom Brown, Samuel S. Hinds, Paul Kelly, Barnett Parker, Frank Albertson.
Released: November 1937.

OF HUMAN HEARTS (1938)
MGM: 105 minutes
Producer: John W. Considine, Jr. *Director*: Clarence Brown. *Screenplay*: Bradbury Foote, from the story 'Benefits Forgot' by Honore Morrow. *Photography*: Clyde DeVinna. *Music*: Herbert Stothart. *Leading players*: Walter Huston, James Stewart, Beulah Bondi, Guy Kibbee, Charles D. Coburn, John Carradine, Ann Rutherford, Charley Grapewin, Leona Roberts.
Released: February 1938.

VIVACIOUS LADY (1938)
RKO: 92 minutes
Producer and director: George Stevens. *Screenplay*: P.J. Wolfson, Ernest Pagano and (uncredited) Ann Morrison Chapin, from a novelette by I.A.R. Wylie. *Photography*: Robert De Grasse. *Music*: Roy Webb. *Leading players*: Ginger Rogers, James Stewart, James Ellison, Charles Coburn, Beulah Bondi, Frances Mercer, Phyllis Kennedy, Franklin Pangborn, Jack Carson, Grady Sutton, Alec Craig.
Released: May 1938.

THE SHOPWORN ANGEL (1938)
MGM: 85 minutes
Producer: Joseph L. Mankiewicz. *Director*: H.C. Potter. *Screenplay*: Waldo Salt and (uncredited) Howard Estabrook, from the story 'Private Pettigrew's Girl' by Dana Burnet. *Photography*: Joseph Ruttenberg. *Music*: Edward Ward. *Leading players*: Margaret Sullavan, James Stewart, Walter Pidgeon, Hattie McDaniel, Nat Pendleton, Alan Curtis, Sam Levene, Eleanor Lynn, Charles D. Brown, Charley Grapewin.
Released: July 1938.

YOU CAN'T TAKE IT WITH YOU (1938)
Columbia: 127 minutes
Producer and Director: Frank Capra. *Screenplay*: Robert Riskin, from the stage play by George S. Kaufman and Moss Hart. *Photography*: Joseph Walker. *Music*: Dimitri Tiomkin. *Leading players*: Jean Arthur, Lionel Barrymore, James Stewart, Edward Arnold, Mischa Auer, Ann Miller, Spring Byington, Samuel S. Hinds, Donald Meek, H.B. Warner, Halliwell Hobbes, Dub Taylor, Mary Forbes.
Released: September 1938.

MADE FOR EACH OTHER (1939)
United Artists: 90 minutes
Producer: David O. Selznick. *Director*: John Cromwell. *Screenplay*: Jo Swerling, from a story idea by Rose Franken. *Photography*: Leon Shamroy. *Music*: Lou Forbes. *Leading players*: Carole Lombard, James Stewart, Charles Coburn, Lucile Watson, Harry Davenport, Ruth Weston, Donald Briggs, Eddie Quillan, Esther Dale.
Released: February 1939.

THE ICE FOLLIES OF 1939 (1939)
MGM: 83 minutes
Producer: Harry Rapf. *Director*: Reinhold Schunzel. *Screenplay*: Leonard Praskins, Florence Ryerson and Edgar Allan Woolf, from a screen story by Praskins. *Photography*: Joseph Ruttenberg; Technicolor sequence by Oliver T. Marsh. *Music Director*: Roger Edens. *Leading players*: Joan Crawford, James Stewart, Lew Ayres, Lewis Stone, Bess Ehrhardt, Lionel Stander, Charles D. Brown, Truman Bradley, Marie Blake.
Released: March 1939.

IT'S A WONDERFUL WORLD (1939)
MGM: 86 minutes
Producer: Frank Davis. *Director*: W.S. Van Dyke II. *Screenplay*: Ben Hecht, from a screen story by Hecht and Herman J. Mankiewicz. *Photography*: Oliver T. Marsh. *Music*: Edward Ward. *Leading players*: Claudette Colbert, James Stewart, Guy Kibbee, Nat Pendleton, Frances Drake, Edgar Kennedy, Ernest Truex, Richard Carle.
Released: May 1939.

MR SMITH GOES TO WASHINGTON (1939)
Columbia: 126 minutes
Producer and Director: Frank Capra. *Screenplay*: Sidney Buchman, from the story 'The Gentleman From Montana' by Lewis R. Foster. *Photography*: Joseph Walker. *Music*: Dimitri Tiomkin. *Leading players*: Jean Arthur, James Stewart, Claude Rains, Edward Arnold, Guy Kibbee, Thomas Mitchell, Eugene Pallette, Beulah Bondi, H.B. Warner, Harry Carey, Astrid Allwyn, Ruth Donnelly, Grant Mitchell, Porter Hall.
Released: October 1939.

DESTRY RIDES AGAIN (1939)
Universal: 94 minutes
Producer: Joe Pasternak. *Director*: George Marshall. *Screenplay:* Felix Jackson, Gertrude Purcell and Henry Myers, from a screen story by Felix Jackson, derived from the novel by Max Brand. *Photography*: Hal Mohr. *Music*: Frank Skinner. *Leading players*: Marlene Dietrich, James Stewart, Mischa Auer, Charles Winninger, Brian Donlevy, Allen Jenkins, Warren Hymer, Irene Hervey, Una Merkel, Billy Gilbert, Samuel S. Hinds, Jack Carson.
Released: December 1939.

THE SHOP AROUND THE CORNER (1940)
MGM: 97 minutes
Producer and director: Ernst Lubitsch. *Screenplay*: Samson Raphaelson and (uncredited) Ben Hecht, from the play 'Perfumerie' by Nicholaus Laszlo. *Photography*: William Daniels. *Music*: Werner R. Heymann. *Leading players*: Margaret Sullavan, James Stewart, Frank Morgan, Joseph Schildkraut, Sara Haden, Felix Bressart, William Tracy, Inez Courtney, Charles Halton, Charles Smith.
Released: January 1940.

THE MORTAL STORM (1940)
MGM: 100 minutes
Producer: Sidney Franklin. *Director*: Frank Borzage. *Screenplay*: Claudine West, Andersen Ellis and George Froeschel, from the novel by Phyllis Bottome. *Photography*: William Daniels. *Music*: Edward Kane. *Leading players*: Margaret Sullavan, James Stewart, Robert Young, Frank Morgan, Robert Stack, Bonita Granville, Irene Rich, William T. Orr, Maria Ouspenskaya, Gene Reynolds, Russell Hicks.
Released: June 1940.

NO TIME FOR COMEDY (1940)
Warner Bros: 93 minutes
Producer: Hal Wallis. *Director*: William Keighley. *Screenplay*: Julius J. and Philip G. Epstein, from the play by S.N. Behrman. *Photography*: Ernest Haller. *Music*: Heinz Roemheld. *Leading players*: James Stewart, Rosalind Russell, Genevieve Tobin, Charlie Ruggles, Allyn Joslyn, Clarence Kolb, Louise Beavers, J.M. Kerrigan.
Released: September 1940.

THE PHILADELPHIA STORY (1940)
MGM: 112 minutes
Producer: Joseph L. Mankiewicz. *Director*: George Cukor. *Screenplay*:
Donald Ogden Stewart and (uncredited) Waldo Salt, from the play by
Philip Barry. *Photography*: Joseph Ruttenberg. *Music*: Franz Waxman.
Leading players: Cary Grant, Katharine Hepburn, James Stewart, Ruth
Hussey, John Howard, Roland Young, John Halliday, Virginia Weidler,
Mary Nash, Henry Daniell, Lionel Pape.
Released: December 1940.

COME LIVE WITH ME (1941)
MGM: 86 minutes
Producer and Director: Clarence Brown. *Screenplay*: Patterson McNutt,
from an original story by Virginia Van Upp. *Photography*: George Folsey.
Music: Herbert Stothart. *Leading players*: James Stewart, Hedy Lamarr,
Ian Hunter, Verree Teasdale, Donald Meek, Barton MacLane, Edward
Ashley, Ann Codee.
Released: January 1941.

POT O' GOLD (1941)
United Artists: 86 minutes
Producer: James Roosevelt. *Director*: George Marshall. *Screenplay*: Walter
De Leon, from a screen story by Monte Brice, Andrew Bennison, and
Harry Tugend, from a story idea by Haydn Roth Evans and Robert
Brilmayer. *Photography*: Hal Mohr. *Music Director*: Lou Forbes. *Leading
players*: James Stewart, Paulette Goddard, Horace Heidt and his Musical
Knights, Charles Winninger, Mary Gordon, Frank Melton, Jed Prouty,
Dick Hogan, James Burke.
Released: April 1941.

ZIEGFELD GIRL (1941)
MGM: 131 minutes
Producer: Pandro S. Berman. *Director*: Robert Z. Leonard. *Screenplay*:
Marguerite Roberts and Sonya Levien, from a story by William
Anthony McGuire. *Photography*: Ray June. *Music*: Herbert Stothart.
Music Director: George Stoll. *Leading players*: James Stewart, Judy
Garland, Hedy Lamarr, Lana Turner, Tony Martin, Jackie Cooper, Ian
Hunter, Charles Winninger, Edward Everett Horton, Philip Dorn, Paul
Kelly, Eve Arden, Dan Dailey Jnr.
Released: April 1941.

IT'S A WONDERFUL LIFE (1946)
RKO: 129 minutes
Producer and Director: Frank Capra. *Screenplay*: Frances Goodrich, Albert
Hackett, based on the story 'The Greatest Gift' by Philip Van Doren
Stern. *Photography*: Joseph Walker & Joseph Biroc. *Music*: Dimitri
Tiomkin. *Leading players*: James Stewart, Donna Reed, Lionel
Barrymore, Thomas Mitchell, Henry Travers, Beulah Bondi, Frank
Faylen, Ward Bond, Gloria Grahame, H.B. Warner, Frank Albertson,
Samuel S. Hinds.
Released: December 1946.

MAGIC TOWN (1947)
RKO: 103 minutes
Producer: Robert Riskin. *Director*: William A. Wellman. *Screenplay*: Robert Riskin, from a screen story by Riskin and Joseph Krumgold. *Photography*: Joseph Biroc. *Music*: Roy Webb. *Leading players*: James Stewart, Jane Wyman, Kent Smith, Ned Sparks, Wallace Ford, Regis Toomey, Ann Doran, Donald Meek.
Released: October 1947.

CALL NORTHSIDE 777 (1948)
20th Century-Fox: 111 minutes
Producer: Otto Lang. *Director*: Henry Hathaway. *Screenplay*: Jerome Cady and Jay Dratler, adapted by Leonard Hoffman and Quentin Reynolds from newspaper articles by James P. McGuire. *Photography*: Joe MacDonald. *Music*: Alfred Newman. *Leading players*: James Stewart, Richard Conte, Lee J. Cobb, Helen Walker, Betty Garde, Kasia Orzazewski, Joanne de Bergh, Howard Smith, Paul Harvey, John McIntire.
Released: February 1948.

ON OUR MERRY WAY (1948)
United Artists: 107 minutes
Producers: Benedict Bogeaus, Burgess Meredith. *Directors*: King Vidor and Leslie Fenton and (uncredited) George Stevens and John Huston. *Screenplay*: Laurence Stallings, Lou Breslow and John O'Hara, from a story by Arch Oboler. *Photography*: John Seitz, Ernest Laszlo & Joseph Biroc. *Music*: Heinz Roemheld. *Leading players*: Paulette Goddard, Burgess Meredith, James Stewart, Henry Fonda, Dorothy Lamour, Victor Moore, Fred MacMurray, William Demarest, Hugh Herbert, Eduardo Ciannelli.
Released: February 1948.

ROPE (1948)
Warner Bros: 80 minutes
Producers: Sidney Bernstein and Alfred Hitchcock. *Director*: Alfred Hitchcock. *Screenplay*: Arthur Laurents and (uncredited) Ben Hecht, adapted by Hume Cronyn from the play by Patrick Hamilton. *Photography*: Joseph Valentine & William V. Skall (Technicolor). *Music director*: Leo F. Forbstein. *Leading players*: James Stewart, John Dall, Farley Granger, Joan Chandler, Cedric Hardwicke, Constance Collier, Edith Evanson, Douglas Dick.
Released: September 1948.

YOU GOTTA STAY HAPPY (1948)
Rampart/Universal-International: 100 minutes
Producer: Karl Tunberg. *Director*: H.C. Potter. *Screenplay*: Karl Tunberg, from a magazine story by Robert Carson. *Photography*: Russell Metty. *Music*: Daniele Amfitheatrof. *Leading players*: Joan Fontaine, James Stewart, Eddie Albert, Roland Young, Willard Parker, Percy Kilbride, Porter Hall, Marcy McGuire.
Released: November 1948.

THE STRATTON STORY (1949)
MGM: 106 minutes
Producer: Jack Cummings. *Director*: Sam Wood. *Screenplay*: Douglas
Morrow, Guy Trosper and (uncredited) George Wells, from a screen
story by Morrow. *Photography*: Harold Rosson. *Music*: Adolph Deutsch.
Leading players: James Stewart, June Allyson, Frank Morgan, Agnes
Moorehead, Bill Williams, Bruce Cowling, Eugene Bearden, Cliff Clark,
Mary Lawrence.
Released: July 1949.

MALAYA (1949)
MGM: 98 minutes
Producer: Edwin Knopf. *Director*: Richard Thorpe. *Screenplay*: Frank
Fenton, from an original story by Manchester Boddy. *Photography*:
George Folsey. *Music*: Bronislau Kaper. *Leading players*: Spencer Tracy,
James Stewart, Valentina Cortesa, Sydney Greenstreet, John Hodiak,
Lionel Barrymore, Gilbert Roland, Roland Winters, Richard Loo, Ian
MacDonald.
Released: December 1949.

WINCHESTER 73 (1950)
Universal-International: 92 minutes
Producer: Aaron Rosenberg. *Director*: Anthony Mann. *Screenplay*: Robert
L. Richards & Borden Chase, from a story by Stuart N. Lake.
Photography: William Daniels. *Music Director*: Joseph Gershenson.
Leading players: James Stewart, Shelley Winters, Dan Duryea, Stephen
McNally, Millard Mitchell, Charles Drake, John McIntire, Will Geer, Jay
C. Flippen, Rock Hudson.
Released: July 1950.

BROKEN ARROW (1950)
20th Century-Fox: 93 minutes
Producer: Julian Blaustein. *Director*: Delmer Daves. *Screenplay*: Michael
Blankfort and (uncredited) Albert Maltz, from the novel 'Blood Brother'
by Elliott Arnold. *Photography*: Ernest Palmer (Technicolor). *Music*:
Hugo Friedhofer. *Leading players*: James Stewart, Jeff Chandler, Debra
Paget, Basil Ruysdael, Will Geer, Joyce MacKenzie, Arthur Hunnicutt,
Raymond Bramley, Jay Silverheels.
Released: August 1950.

THE JACKPOT (1950)
20th Century-Fox: 87 minutes
Producer: Samuel G. Engel. *Director*: Walter Lang. *Screenplay*: Phoebe &
Henry Ephron, from a magazine article by John McNulty. *Photography*:
Joseph LaShelle. *Music*: Lionel Newman. *Leading players*: James Stewart,
Barbara Hale, James Gleason, Fred Clark, Alan Mowbray, Patricia
Medina, Natalie Wood, Tommy Rettig, Robert Gist, Lyle Talbot, Charles
Tannen.
Released: November 1950.

HARVEY (1950)
Universal-International: 104 minutes
Producer: John Beck. *Director*: Henry Koster. *Screenplay*: Mary Chase & Oscar Brodney, from the stage play by Chase. *Photography*: William Daniels. *Music*: Frank Skinner. *Leading players*: James Stewart, Josephine Hull, Peggy Dow, Charles Drake, Cecil Kellaway, Victoria Horne, Jesse White, William Lynn, Wallace Ford, Nana Bryant.
Released: December 1950.

NO HIGHWAY (1951)
20th Century-Fox: 99 minutes
Producer: Louis D. Lighton. *Director*: Henry Koster. *Screenplay*: R.C. Sherriff, Oscar Millard and Alec Coppel, from the novel by Nevil Shute. *Photography*: Georges Perinal. *Leading players*: James Stewart, Marlene Dietrich, Glynis Johns, Jack Hawkins, Janette Scott, Ronald Squire, Elizabeth Allan, Niall MacGinnis, Kenneth More, Jill Clifford, David Hutcheson, Wilfrid Hyde White.
Released: August 1951.

THE GREATEST SHOW ON EARTH (1952)
Paramount: 153 minutes
Producer and Director: Cecil B. DeMille. *Screenplay*: Frederic M. Frank, Barre Lyndon and Theodore St John, from a screen story by Frank St. John and Frank Cavett. *Photography*: Georges Barnes (Technicolor). *Music*: Victor Young. *Leading players*: Betty Hutton, Cornel Wilde, Charlton Heston, Dorothy Lamour, Gloria Grahame, James Stewart, Lyle Bettger, Henry Wilcoxon, Lawrence Tierney, Emmett Kelly.
Released: January 1952.

BEND OF THE RIVER (1952)
Universal-International: 91 minutes
Producer: Aaron Rosenberg. *Director*: Anthony Mann. *Screenplay*: Borden Chase, from the novel by Bill Gulick. *Photography*: Irving Glassberg (Technicolor). *Music*: Hans J. Salter. *Leading players*: James Stewart, Arthur Kennedy, Julia Adams, Rock Hudson, Lori Nelson, Jay C. Flippen, Chubby Johnson, Henry 'Harry' Morgan, Royal Dano, Frances Bavier, Howard Petrie, Stepin Fetchit, Jack Lambert.
Release: January 1952.

CARBINE WILLIAMS (1952)
MGM: 91 minutes
Producer: Armand Deutsch. *Director*: Richard Thorpe. *Screenplay*: Art Cohn, from a non-fiction magazine feature by David Marshall Williams. *Photography*: William Mellor. *Music*: Conrad Salinger. *Leading players*: James Stewart, Jean Hagen, Wendell Corey, Carl Benton Reid, Paul Stewart, Otto Hulett, Rhys Williams, Herbert Heyes, James Arness, Porter Hall.
Released: May 1952.

THE NAKED SPUR (1953)
MGM: 91 minutes
Producer: William H. Wright. *Director*: Anthony Mann. *Screenplay*: Sam Rolfe & Harold Jack Bloom. *Photography*: William C. Mellor (Color). *Music*: Bronislau Kaper. *Leading players*: James Stewart, Robert Ryan, Janet Leigh, Ralph Meeker, Millard Mitchell.
Released: February 1953.

THUNDER BAY (1953)
Universal-International: 102 minutes
Producer: Aaron Rosenberg. *Director*: Anthony Mann. *Screenplay*: Gil Doud & John Michael Hayes & (uncredited) Borden Chase, from a screen story by Hayes, based on an idea by George W. George and George F. Slavin. *Photography*: William Daniels (Technicolor). *Music*: Frank Skinner. *Leading players*: James Stewart, Joanne Dru, Gilbert Roland, Dan Duryea, Marcia Henderson, Jay C. Flippen, Antonio Moreno, Robert Monet, Henry 'Harry' Morgan.
Released: August 1953.

THE GLENN MILLER STORY (1953)
Universal-International: 116 minutes
Producer: Aaron Rosenberg. *Director*: Anthony Mann. *Screenplay*: Valentine Davies & Oscar Broadney. *Photography*: William Daniels (Technicolor). *Music Direction*: Joseph Gershenson. *Leading players*: James Stewart, June Allyson, Henry 'Harry' Morgan, Charles Drake, George Tobias, Barton MacLane, Sig Ruman, Irving Bacon, James Bell, Kathleen Lockhart, Katharine Warren, Frances Langford, Louis Armstrong, Ben Pollack, Gene Krupa.
Released: December 1953.

REAR WINDOW (1954)
Paramount: 112 minutes
Producer and Director: Alfred Hitchcock. *Screenplay*: John Michael Hayes, from the short story by Cornell Woolrich. *Photography*: Robert Burks (Technicolor). *Music*: Franz Waxman. *Leading players*: James Stewart, Grace Kelly, Wendell Corey, Thelma Ritter, Raymond Burr, Judith Evelyn, Ross Bagdasarian.
Released: September 1954.

THE FAR COUNTRY (1955)
Universal-International: 97 minutes
Producer: Aaron Rosenberg. *Director*: Anthony Mann. *Screenplay*: Borden Chase. *Photography*: William Daniels (Technicolor). *Music*: Hans J. Salter. *Leading players*: James Stewart, Ruth Roman, Corinne Calvert, Walter Brennan, John McIntire, Jay C. Flippen, Henry 'Harry' Morgan, Steve Brodie, Royal Dano, Connie Gilchrist, Kathleen Freeman, Bob Wilke.
Released: February 1955.

STRATEGIC AIR COMMAND (1955)
Paramount: 114 minutes
Producer: Samuel J. Briskin. *Director*: Anthony Mann. *Screenplay*:
Valentine Davies & Beirne Lay Jr., from a screen story by Lay.
Photography: William Daniels (Technicolor/VistaVision). *Music*: Victor
Young. *Leading players*: James Stewart, June Allyson, Frank Lovejoy,
Barry Sullivan, Alex Nicol, James Millican, Bruce Bennett, Jay C.
Flippen, James Bell, Rosemary DeCamp.
Released: April 1955.

THE MAN FROM LARAMIE (1955)
Columbia: 104 minutes
Producer: William Goetz. *Director*: Anthony Mann. *Screenplay*: Philip
Yordan & Frank Burt, from the magazine serial and novel by Thomas T.
Flynn. *Photography*: Charles Lang (Technicolor/CinemaScope). *Music*:
George Duning. *Leading players*: James Stewart, Arthur Kennedy,
Donald Crisp, Cathy O'Donnell, Alex Nicol, Aline MacMahon, Wallace
Ford, Jack Elam, John War Eagle, James Millican.
Released: August 1955.

THE MAN WHO KNEW TOO MUCH (1956)
Paramount: 120 minutes
Producer and Director: Alfred Hitchcock. *Screenplay*: John Michael Hayes
& Angus McPhail, from a story by Charles Bennett & D.B. Wyndham-
Lewis. *Photography*: Robert Burks (Technicolor/VistaVision). *Music*:
Bernard Herrmann. *Leading players*: James Stewart, Doris Day, Brenda
de Banzie, Bernard Miles, Ralph Truman, Daniel Gelin, Mogens Wieth,
Alan Mowbray, Richard Wattis, Reggie Nalder.
Released: June 1956.

THE SPIRIT OF ST LOUIS (1957)
Warner Bros: 135 minutes
Producer: Leland Hayward. *Director*: Billy Wilder. *Screenplay*: Billy
Wilder & Wendell Mayes, adapted by Charles Lederer from the book by
Charles A. Lindbergh. *Photography*: Robert Burks & J. Peverell Marley
(WarnerColor/CinemaScope). *Music*: Franz Waxman. *Leading players*:
James Stewart, Murray Hamilton, Patricia Smith, Barlett Robinson,
Marc Connelly, Arthur Space, Charles Watts.
Released: April 1957.

NIGHT PASSAGE (1957)
Universal-International: 90 minutes
Producer: Aaron Rosenberg. *Director*: James Neilson. *Screenplay*: Borden
Chase, from the novel by Norman A. Fox. *Photography*: William Daniels
(Technicolor/Technirama). *Music*: Dimitri Tiomkin. *Leading players*:
James Stewart, Audie Murphy, Dan Duryea, Dianne Foster, Elaine
Stewart, Brandon de Wilde, Jay C. Flippen, Herbert Anderson, Robert J.
Wilke, Hugh Beaumont, Jack Elam.
Released: May 1957.

VERTIGO (1958)
Paramount: 128 minutes
Producer and Director: Alfred Hitchcock. *Screenplay*: Alec Coppel & Samuel Taylor, from the novel 'D'Entre Les Morts/From Among the Dead' by Pierre Boileau and Thomas Narcejac. *Photography*: Robert Burks (Technicolor/VistaVision). *Music*: Bernard Herrmann. *Leading players*: James Stewart, Kim Novak, Barbara Bel Geddes, Tom Helmore, Henry Jones, Raymond Bailey, Ellen Corby, Konstantin Shayne.
Released: May 1958.

BELL, BOOK AND CANDLE (1958)
Columbia: 103 minutes
Producer: Julian Blaustein. *Director*: Richard Quine. *Screenplay*: Daniel Taradash, from the play by John Van Druten. *Photography*: James Wong Howe (Technicolor). *Music*: George Duning. *Leading players*: James Stewart, Kim Novak, Jack Lemmon, Ernie Kovacs, Hermione Gingold, Elsa Lanchester, Janice Rule, Howard McNear.
Released: December 1958.

ANATOMY OF A MURDER (1959)
Columbia: 160 minutes
Producer and Director: Otto Preminger. *Screenplay*: Wendell Mayes, from the novel by Robert Traver. *Photography*: Sam Leavitt. *Music*: Duke Ellington. *Leading players*: James Stewart, Lee Remick, Ben Gazzara, Joseph N. Welch, Kathryn Grant, Arthur O'Connell, Eve Arden, George C. Scott, Brooks West, Orson Bean, John Qualen, Murray Hamilton, Russ Brown.
Released: July 1959.

THE FBI STORY (1959)
Warner Bros: 149 minutes
Producer and Director: Mervyn LeRoy. *Screenplay*: Richard L. Breen & John Twist, from the book by Don Whitehead. *Photography*: Joseph Biroc (Technicolor). *Music*: Max Steiner. *Leading players*: James Stewart, Vera Miles, Murray Hamilton, Larry Pennell, Nick Adams, Diane Jergens, Jean Willes, Joyce Taylor, Victor Millan, Parley Baer.
Released: October 1959.

THE MOUNTAIN ROAD (1960)
Columbia: 102 minutes
Producer: William Goetz. *Director*: Daniel Mann. *Screenplay*: Alfred Hayes, from the novel by Theodore H. White. *Photography*: Burnett Guffey. *Music*: Jerome Moross. *Leading players*: James Stewart, Lisa Lu, Glenn Corbett, Henry 'Harry' Morgan, Frank Silvera, James Best, Rudy Bond, Mike Kellin, Frank Maxwell.
Released: June 1960.

TWO RODE TOGETHER (1961)
Columbia: 109 minutes

Producer: Stan Shpetner. *Director*: John Ford. *Screenplay*: Frank Nugent, from the magazine serial and novel 'Comanche Captives' by Will Cook. *Photography*: Charles Lawton Jr. (Eastman Color by Pathe). *Music*: George Duning. *Leading players*: James Stewart, Richard Widmark, Shirley Jones, Linda Cristal, Andy Devine, John McIntire, Paul Birch, Willis Bouchey, Henry Brandon, Harry Carey Jr, Olive Carey, Ken Curtis.
Released: July 1961.

THE MAN WHO SHOT LIBERTY VALANCE (1962)
Paramount: 122 minutes
Producer: Willis Goldbeck. *Director*: John Ford. *Screenplay*: Willis Goldbeck & James Warner Bellah, from the short story by Dorothy M. Johnson. *Photography*: William H. Clothier. *Music*: Cyril J. Mockridge. *Leading players*: James Stewart, John Wayne, Vera Miles, Lee Marvin, Edmond O'Brien, Andy Devine, Ken Murray, John Carradine, Jeanette Nolan, John Qualen, Willis Bouchey, Carleton Young, Woody Strode, Denver Pyle, Strother Martin, Lee Van Cleef.
Released: April 1962.

MR HOBBS TAKES A VACATION (1962)
20th Century-Fox: 116 minutes
Producer: Jerry Wald. *Director*: Henry Koster. *Screenplay*: Nunnally Johnson, from the novel 'Mr Hobbs' Vacation' by Edward Streeter. *Photography*: William C. Mellor (DeLuxe Color/CinemaScope). *Music*: Henry Mancini. *Leading players*: James Stewart, Maureen O'Hara, Fabian, Lauri Peters, Lili Gentle, John Saxon, John McGiver, Marie Wilson, Reginald Gardiner, Valerie Varda, Natalie Trundy.
Released: June 1962.

HOW THE WEST WAS WON (1962)
MGM: 162 minutes
Producer: Bernard Smith. *Directors*: John Ford, Henry Hathaway & George Marshall. *Screenplay*: James R. Webb & (uncredited) John Gay, based on the 'Life' magazine series. *Photography*: Joseph LaShelle, Charles Lang Jr, William Daniels, Milton Krasner (Metrocolor/ Cinerama). *Music*: Alfred Newman. *Leading players*: Carroll Baker, Lee J. Cobb, Henry Fonda, Carolyn Jones, Karl Malden, Gregory Peck, George Peppard, Robert Preston, Debbie Reynolds, James Stewart, Eli Wallach, John Wayne, Richard Widmark.
Released: November 1962.

TAKE HER, SHE'S MINE (1963)
20th Century-Fox: 98 minutes
Producer and Director: Henry Koster. *Screenplay*: Nunnally Johnson, from the play by Phoebe and Henry Ephron. *Photography*: Lucien Ballard (DeLuxe Color/CinemaScope). *Music*: Jerry Goldsmith. *Leading players*: James Stewart, Sandra Dee, Audrey Meadows, Robert Morley, Philippe Forquet, John McGiver, Robert Denver, Monica Moran.
Released: November 1963.

CHEYENNE AUTUMN (1964)
Warner Bros: 161 minutes
Producer: Bernard Smith. *Director*: John Ford. *Screenplay*: James R. Webb,
from the novel by Mari Sandoz. *Photography*: William H. Clothier
(Technicolor/Super Panavision 70). *Music*: Alex North. *Leading players*:
Richard Widmark, Carroll Baker, Karl Malden, Sal Mineo, Dolores Del
Rio, Ricardo Montalban, Gilbert Roland, Arthur Kennedy, James
Stewart, Edward G. Robinson, Patrick Wayne, Elizabeth Allen, John
Carradine, Victor Jory.
Released: October 1964.

DEAR BRIGITTE (1965)
20th Century-Fox: 100 minutes
Producer and Director: Henry Koster. *Screenplay*: Hal Kanter and
(uncredited) Nunnally Johnson, from the novel 'Erasmus With
Freckles' by John Haase. *Photography*: Lucien Ballard (DeLuxe
Color/CinemaScope). *Music*: George Duning. *Leading players*: James
Stewart, Fabian, Glynis Johns, Cindy Carol, Billy Mumy, John Williams,
Jack Kruschen, Ed Wynn, Charles Robinson, Howard Freeman.
Released: January 1965.

SHENANDOAH (1965)
Universal: 105 minutes
Producer: Robert Arthur. *Director*: Andrew V. McLaglen. *Screenplay*:
James Lee Barrett. *Photography*: William H. Clothier (Technicolor).
Music: Frank Skinner. *Leading players*: James Stewart, Doug McClure,
Glenn Corbett, Patrick Wayne, Rosemary Forsyth, Phillip Alford,
Katharine Ross, Charles Robinson, James McMullan, Tim McIntire,
George Kennedy, Strother Martin.
Released: June 1965.

THE FLIGHT OF THE PHOENIX (1965)
20th Century-Fox: 147 minutes.
Producer and Director: Robert Aldrich. *Screenplay*: Lukas Heller, from the
novel by Elleston Trevor. *Photography*: Joseph Biroc (DeLuxe Color).
Music: De Vol. *Leading players*: James Stewart, Richard Attenborough,
Peter Finch, Hardy Kruger, Ernest Borgnine, Ian Bannen, Ronald
Fraser, Christian Marquand, Dan Duryea, George Kennedy.
Released: December 1965.

THE RARE BREED (1966)
Universal: 97 minutes
Producer: William Alland. *Director*: Andrew V. McLaglen. *Screenplay*: Ric
Hardman. *Photography*: William H. Clothier (Technicolor/Panavision).
Music: Johnny Williams. *Leading players*: James Stewart, Maureen
O'Hara, Brian Keith, Juliet Mills, Don Galloway, David Brian, Jack
Elam, Ben Johnson, Harry Carey Jr, Perry Lopez.
Released: February 1966.

FIRECREEK (1968)
Warner Bros/Seven Arts: 104 minutes
Producer: Philip Leacock. *Director*: Vincent McEveety. *Screenplay*:
Calvin Clements. *Photography*: William H. Clothier (Technicolor/
Panavision). *Music*: Alfred Newman. *Leading players*: James Stewart,
Henry Fonda, Inger Stevens, Gary Lockwood, Dean Jagger, Ed Begley,
Jay C. Flippen, Jack Elam, James Best.
Released: January 1968.

BANDOLERO! (1968)
20th Century-Fox: 106 minutes
Producer: Robert L. Jacks. *Director*: Andrew V. McLaglen. *Screenplay*:
James Lee Barrett, from a screen story by Stanley L. Hough.
Photography: William H. Clothier (DeLuxe Color/Panavision). *Music*:
Jerry Goldsmith. *Leading players*: James Stewart, Dean Martin, Raquel
Welch, George Kennedy, Andrew Prine, Will Geer, Clint Ritchie,
Denver Pyle, Tom Heaton.
Released: June 1968.

THE CHEYENNE SOCIAL CLUB (1970)
National General Pictures: 103 minutes
Producer and Director: Gene Kelly. *Screenplay*: James Lee Barrett.
Photography: William H. Clothier (Technicolor/Panavision). *Music*:
Walter Scharf. *Leading players*: James Stewart, Henry Fonda, Shirley
Jones, Sue Anne Langdon, Elaine Devry, Robert Middleton, Arch
Johnson, Dabbs Greer, Jackie Russell.
Released: June 1970.

FOOL'S PARADE (1971)
Columbia: 98 minutes
Producer and Director: Andrew V. McLaglen. *Screenplay*: James Lee
Barrett, from the novel by Davis Grubb. *Photography*: Harry Stradling Jr
(Eastman color). *Music*: Henry Vars. *Leading players*: James Stewart,
George Kennedy, Anne Baxter, Strother Martin, Kurt Russell, William
Windom, Mike Kellin, Kathy Cannon, Morgan Paull, Robert Donner.
Released: July 1971.

THE SHOOTIST (1976)
Paramount: 100 minutes
Producers: M.J. Frankovich & William Self. *Director*: Don Siegel.
Screenplay: Miles Hood Swarthout & Scott Hale, from the novel by
Glendon Swarthout. *Photography*: Bruce Surtees (Technicolor). *Music*:
Elmer Bernstein. *Leading players*: John Wayne, Lauren Bacall, Ron
Howard, James Stewart, Richard Boone, Hugh O'Brian, Bill McKinney,
Harry Morgan, John Carradine, Sheree North, Richard Lenz, Scatman
Crothers.
Released: August 1976.

AIRPORT '77 (1977)
Universal: 114 minutes
Producer: William Frye. *Director*: Jerry Jameson. *Screenplay*: Michael
Scheff, David Spector, from a screen story by H.A.L. Craig & Charles
Kuenstle inspired by the film *Airport* based on the novel by Arthur
Hailey. *Photography*: Philip Lathrop (Technicolor/Panavision). *Music*:
John Cacavas. *Leading players*: Jack Lemmon, Lee Grant, Brenda
Vaccaro, Joseph Cotten, Olivia de Havilland, Darren McGavin,
Christopher Lee, George Kennedy, James Stewart.
Released: March 1977.

THE BIG SLEEP (1978)
ITC: 99 minutes
Producers: Elliott Kastner & Michael Winner. *Direction and Screenplay*:
Michael Winner, from the novel by Raymond Chandler. *Photography*:
Robert Paynter (DeLuxe color). *Music*: Jerry Fielding. *Leading players*:
Robert Mitchum, Sarah Miles, Richard Boone, Candy Clark, Joan
Collins, Edward Fox, John Mills, James Stewart, Oliver Reed, Harry
Andrews, Colin Blakely, Richard Todd.
Released: March 1978.

THE MAGIC OF LASSIE (1978)
International Picture Show/Lassie Productions: 99 minutes
Producers: Bonita Granville Wrather & William Beaudine Jr. *Director*:
Don Chaffey. *Screenplay*: Jean Holloway, Richard M. Sherman & Robert
B. Sherman, from a screenstory by the Shermans. *Photography*: Michael
Margulies (colour). *Music*: Irwin Kostal. *Leading players*: James Stewart,
Mickey Rooney, Pernell Roberts, Stephanie Zimbalist, Michael Sharrett,
Alice Faye, Gene Evans, Mike Mazurki, Robert Lussier, Lane Davies,
William Flatley.
Released: August 1978.

THE GREEN HORIZON (1981)
Sanrio Communications: 87 minutes
Producers: Terry Ogisu & Yoichi Matsue. *Directors*: Susumu Hani &
Simon Trevor. *Screenplay*: Shintaro Tsuji, from a screen story by Shuji
Terayama. *Photography*: Simon Trevor & Tsuguzo Matsumae (DeLuxe
color). *Music Director*: Naozumi Yamamoto. *Leading players*: James
Stewart, Philip Sayer, Cathleen McOsker, Eleonora Vallone, Hakuta
Simba, Michael Clark, Mike Simochelo.
Released: November 1981.

AN AMERICAN TAIL: FIEVEL GOES WEST (1991)
Universal: 74 minutes
Producers: Steven Spielberg & Robert Watts. *Directors*: Phil Nibbelink
& Simon Wells. *Screenplay*: Flint Dille, from a story by Charles Swenson.
Music: James Horner. *Cartoon Voices*: Dom DeLuise (Tiger), James
Stewart (Wylie Burp), John Cleese (Cat R. Waul), Amy Irving (Miss
Kitty), Phillip Glasser (Fievel Mousekewitz), Cathy Cavadini (Tanya
Mousekewitz), Nehemiah Persoff (Poppa Mousekewitz).
Released: November 1991.

Television Work

THE WINDMILL (1955)
CBS: 30 minutes. Featuring James Stewart, Barbara Hale, Donald MacDonald, Cheryl Callaway, John McIntire, Walter Sande, James Millican.

THE TOWN WITH A PAST (1957)
CBS: 30 minutes/G.E. Theater Series. Featuring James Stewart, Fredd Wayne, Walter Sande, Ted Mapes. Introduced by Ronald Reagan.

THE TRAIL TO CHRISTMAS (1957)
CBS: 30 minutes/G.E. Theater Series. Directed by James Stewart. Featuring Stewart, Richard Eyer, John McIntire, Sam Edwards, Will Wright, Kevin Hagen, Sally Frazier.

CINDY'S FELLA (1959)
NBC: 53 minutes/Lincoln-Mercury. Startime television series. Featuring James Stewart, George Gobel, Lois Smith, James Best, Mary Wickes, Kathie Browne, Alice Backes, George Keymas.

FLASHING SPIKES (1962)
Avista: 53 minutes/Alcoa Premiere. American television series. Featuring James Stewart, Jack Warden, Pat Wayne, Edgar Buchanan, Tige Andrews, Carleton Young, Willis Bouchey, Don Drysdale.

THE JIMMY STEWART SHOW (1971)
A weekly thirty-minute comedy series produced by Warner Bros and transmitted on NBC network for 24 consecutive episodes. Leading players: James Stewart, Julie Adams, Jonathan Daly, Ellen Geer, Kirby Furlong, Dennis Larson, John McGiver.

HARVEY (1972)
NBC: 90 minutes/Hallmark Hall Of Fame series. Directed by Fielder Cook and adapted by Jacqueline Babbin & Audrey Gellen Maas from the play by Mary Chase. Featuring James Stewart, Helen Hayes, Marian Hailey, John McGiver, Richard Mulligan, Jesse White, Arlene Francis, Madeline Kahn.

HAWKINS ON MURDER (1973)
Arena/Leda/MGM: 90 minutes/CBS. Directed by Jud Taylor. Featuring James Stewart, Strother Martin, Bonnie Bedelia, Kate Reid, David Huddleston, Dana Elcar, Antoinette Bower, Charles McGraw, Robert Webber.

HAWKINS: MURDER IN MOVIELAND (1973)
90 minutes. Directed by Jud Taylor. Featuring James Stewart, Sheree North, Cameron Mitchell, Strother Martin, William Smithers, Kenneth Mars, Maggie Wellman.

HAWKINS: DIE, DARLING DIE (1973)
90 minutes. Directed by Paul Wendkos. Featuring James Stewart, Julie Harris, Mayf Nutter, Diana Douglas, Murray Hamilton, Henry Jones, Sam Elliott, Judson Morgan.

HAWKINS: A LIFE FOR A LIFE (1973)
90 minutes. Directed by Jud Taylor. Featuring James Stewart, William Windom, John Ventantonio, James Hampton, Noam Pitlik, Tyne Daly, Jeanne Cooper.

HAWKINS: BLOOD FEUD (1973)
90 minutes. Directed by Paul Wendkos. Featuring James Stewart, Lew Ayres, Strother Martin, Richard Kelton, Mayf Nutter, James Best, Diana Ewing, Jeanette Nolan.

HAWKINS: MURDER IN THE SLAVE TRADE (1974)
90 minutes. Directed by Paul Wendkos. Featuring James Stewart, Mayf Nutter, Ellen Weston, Peter Mark Richman, James Luisi, Joseph Hindy, Dick Gautier, Warren Kemmerling, Robert Sampson.

HAWKINS: MURDER ON THE 13TH FLOOR (1974)
90 minutes. Directed by Jud Taylor. Featuring James Stewart, Strother Martin, Teresa Wright, Andrew Parks, Albert Paulsen, Herb Edelman, Signe Hasso, Kurt Kaznar, Jeff Corey.

HAWKINS: CANDIDATE FOR MURDER (1974)
90 minutes. Directed by Robert Scheerer. Featuring James Stewart, Strother Martin, Paul Burke, Diana Hyland, Andrew Prine, John Ericson, Mark Gordon, Pernell Roberts.

MR KRUEGER'S CHRISTMAS (1980)
30 minutes. Sponsored by the Mormon Church; directed by Keith Merrill. Featuring James Stewart and The Mormon Tabernacle Choir.

RIGHT OF WAY (1983)
Schaefer/Karpf, Post-Newsweek Video, Home Box Office: 106 minutes. Directed by George Schaefer from a screenplay by Richard Lees (from his play). Featuring James Stewart, Bette Davis, Melinda Dillon,

Priscilla Morrill, John Harkins, Louis Schaefer, Lynn Colton, Charles Walker.

NORTH AND SOUTH, BOOK 2 (1986)
ABC/Warner. Mini-series about two families and their lives up to and including the Civil War. Stewart featured in a cameo as a Southern lawyer.

Stewart has also narrated or appeared as himself in the following films.

FELLOW AMERICANS (1942) A documentary dramatising the implications of the Japanese attack on Pearl Harbor. Directed by Garson Kanin from a screenplay by Robert W. Russell. Office Of Emergency Management (10 minutes).

WINNING YOUR WINGS (1942) A short about the Army Air Corps. Produced by the Office of War Information.

THE AMERICAN CREED (1946) Produced by David Selznick.

THUNDERBOLT (1947) Introduced by James Stewart, a documentary about fighter plane support of ground troops. Director/William Wyler. Technicolor. 44 minutes.

10,000 KIDS AND A COP (1948 Documentary)

HOW MUCH DO YOU OWE? (1949) Documentary for the Disabled American Veterans. Distributed by Columbia. 9 minutes.

AND THEN THERE WERE FOUR (1950) Documentary about road safety. Director: Frank Strayer. Production company: Roland Reed Productions for Socony-Vacuum Oil Company. 27 minutes.

AMBASSADORS WITH WINGS (1958) Production Company: Robert J. Enders Inc for the Ex-Cello Corp. 25 minutes.

X-15 (1961) A missile base drama, directed by Richard Donner, starring Charles Bronson, Ralph Taeger and Brad Dexter and narrated by James Stewart.

DIRECTED BY JOHN FORD (1971) The American Film Institute; a documentary on Ford made by Peter Bogdanovich. Includes an interview with James Stewart.

THE AMERICAN WEST OF JOHN FORD (1971) Documentary on Ford for CBS. Includes interview with James Stewart.

PAT NIXON: PORTRAIT OF A FIRST LADY (1972) A personal look at Mrs Richard M. Nixon during her years as First Lady. Produced by David

Wolper for the Republican Party and narrated by Stewart.

THAT'S ENTERTAINMENT (1974) Musical compilation of the great years of MGM's most successful musicals. Stewart served as one of the star narrators. The film also included an extract from *Born to Dance* with Stewart singing 'Easy To Love'.

SENTIMENTAL JOURNEY (1976) A documentary commemorating the 40th anniversary of the DC-3 aircraft (20 minutes).

Bibliography

Allyson, June (with Frances Spatz Leighton), *June Allyson*, (New York, G.P. Putnam's Sons, 1982)

Capra, Frank, *The Name Above the Title: An Autobiography* (London, W.H. Allen, 1972)

Dietrich, Marlene, *My Life* (London, Weidenfeld & Nicolson, 1989)

Eyles, Allen, *James Stewart* (London, W.H. Allen, 1984)

Ford, Dan, *The Unquiet Man: The Life of John Ford* (London, William Kimber, 1982)

Hayward, Brooke, *Haywire* (New York, Alfred A. Knopf, 1977)

Higham, Charles, *Marlene: The Life of Marlene Dietrich* (New York, W.W. Norton, 1977)

Hotchner, A.E., *Doris Day: Her Own Story* (London, W.H. Allen, 1976)

Hunter, Allan, *James Stewart* (London, Spellmount Ltd, 1985)

Kobal, John, *The Art of the Great Hollywood Portrait Photographers 1925-1940* (London, Allen Lane, 1980)

Logan, Joshua, *Josh: My Up and Down, In and Out Life* (London, W.H. Allen, 1977)

McClure, Arthur F, Jones, Ken D, and Twomey, Alfred E., *The Films of James Stewart* (New York, A.S. Barnes, 1970)

Parish, James Robert and Stanke, Don E., *The All-Americans* (New Rochelle, New York, Arlington House, 1977)

Robbins, Jhan., *Everybody's Man: A Biography of James Stewart* (London, Robson, 1985)

Spoto, Donald, *The Life of Alfred Hitchcock: The Dark Side of Genius* (London, Collins, 1983)

Taylor, John Russell, *Hitch: The Life and Work of Alfred Hitchcock* (London, Faber & Faber, 1978)

Teichmann, Howard, *Fonda: My Life as Told To Howard Teichmann* (London, W.H. Allen, 1982)

Thomas, Tony, *A Wonderful Life: The Films and Career of James Stewart* (New York, Citadel Press, 1988)

Truffaut, Francois, *Hitchcock* (London, Secker & Warburg, 1968)

Westmore, Frank (with Muriel Davidson), *The Westmores of Hollywood* (New York, J.B. Lippincott, 1976)

Willis, Donald C., *The Films of Frank Capra* (Metuchen, New Jersey, Scarecrow Press, 1974)

Index